BROOKLYN TRAVEL GUIDE 2023

An Expert Guide to Brooklyn's Hidden Gems

KATIE ORDELL

Copyright © 2023 Katie Ordell

All rights reserved.

No part of this book may be reproduced, stored in a retrieval system, or transmitted in any form or by any means, electronic, mechanical, photocopying, recording, scanning, or otherwise, without the prior written permission of the publisher.

Table Of Content

INTRODUCTION — 6

CHAPTER ONE: ABOUT BROOKLYN — 8

HISTORY — 8
GEOGRAPHY — 11
CULTURE — 12

CHAPTER TWO: PLANNING YOUR TRIP — 14

WHY VISIT BROOKLYN — 14
BEST TIME TO VISIT BROOKLYN — 16
GETTING TO BROOKLYN — 18

CHAPTER THREE: NEIGHBORHOODS OF BROOKLYN — 20

WILLIAMSBURG — 20
GREEN POINT — 30
BUSHWICK — 38

PARK SLOPE	46
BROOKLYN HEIGHTS	57
DUMBO	64
RED HOOK	70

CHAPTER FOUR: ATTRACTIONS IN BROOKLYN — 78

BROOKLYN BRIDGE	78
PROSPECT PARK	79
BROOKLYN MUSEUM	81
BARCLAYS CENTER	81
BROOKLYN BOTANIC GARDEN	82
BROOKLYN FLEA MARKET	83
INDUSTRIAL CITY	84

CHAPTER FIVE: FOOD AND DRINK IN BROOKLYN — 86

8 BROOKLYN FOODS YOU MUST TRY ONCE IN YOUR LIFE	86
CRAFT BEER AND BREWERIES	91
BRUNCH SPOTS	104

CHAPTER SIX: SHOPPING IN BROOKLYN — 110

INDEPENDENT BOUTIQUES 110
VINTAGE SHOPS 114
BOOKSTORES 122
FLEA MARKETS 132

CHAPTER SEVEN: EVENTS AND FESTIVALS IN BROOKLYN 140

BROOKLYN BOOK FESTIVAL 140
BROOKLYN FILM FESTIVAL 141
FESTIVAL OF AFRO-PUNK 142
SMORGASBURG 144

CHAPTER 8: PRACTICAL INFORMATION FOR VISITORS 148

GETTING AROUND BROOKLYN 148
ACCOMMODATIONS IN BROOKLYN 150
SAFETY TIPS FOR VISITORS 160
MONEY-SAVING TIPS FOR VISITORS 162

CONCLUSION 164

5|BROOKLYN TRAVEL GUIDE 2023

Introduction

In the creative psyche of Americans, Brooklyn occupies a unique place. The Brooklyn Extension, Coney Island, Fulton's Ship, and the Dodgers are just a few otherworldly names connected to the precinct's collection of experiences; each conjures up 1,000 astonishing images illustrating the American experience.

In addition, it embodies the idea of a typical settlement metropolis. The streets of Brooklyn are where one in seven Americans can trace their ancestry. Today, the Creole, Arabic, Spanish, Chinese, and Korean accents of most contemporary Americans can be heard on the roadways of the precinct. If Brooklyn were still unoccupied, it would be the fourth most congested city in the US. The largest of New York City's five precincts, with a population of only 2.3 million, is why it is most well-known, all other things being equal.

7 | BROOKLYN TRAVEL GUIDE 2023

Chapter One: About Brooklyn

History

Despite being a district of New York City for a significant portion of its history, Brooklyn had a long and storied history as a free city before that. In 1890, when Brooklyn was not yet a part of the country, it was classified as the fourth-largest city in the country. In 1636, a group of Dutch ranchers who established a firm foothold along the shore of Gowanus Narrows occupied much of what is now

Brooklyn. The development of Flatlands on Jamaica Straight and Walkabout took place at the same time. A ship to Manhattan was built there in 1642, at the foot of Fulton Road, and the area that grew there became known as The Ship. In 1645, a hamlet was founded not far from where the district lobby is now, and it was given the name Breuckelen, perhaps in honor of a Dutch town. The spelling changed for over a century until Brooklyn became the preferred version.

The crucial Clash of Long Island during the Progressive War occurred in Brooklyn. Post Putnam was built in 1776 by Broad Nathanael Green to safeguard General Washington's retreat after the fight. Americans constructed an earthworks fortress nearby to protect themselves from an English invasion during the War of 1812. They renamed it Stronghold Greene after Broad Greene. In 1846, Walt Whitman, who would eventually become perhaps one of America's most famous authors, managed the Brooklyn Day-to-Day Falcon.

Whitman received the land he requested from Brooklyn, including the Post Greene neighborhood, which was ultimately developed into Stronghold Greene Park, Brooklyn's most well-known park, in 1847. Construction of Frederick Regulation Olmsted's Prospect Park began in 1866.

Leonard Bernstein, a famous author and tour guide, and Mae West, an actor and comedian, were both born in Brooklyn. Throughout the nineteenth century, Brooklyn progressively engulfed neighboring areas, including consolidated towns like Williamsburg, until it reached both sides of the Lord's Region. 1898 it abandoned its unrestricted presence and changed into a New York City district. In 1883, Brooklyn and Manhattan were joined by the Brooklyn Scaffold, one of the wonders of its day in terms of architecture.

The Verrazano-Strait Scaffold connects Staten Island and Brooklyn. At the time, it was still the longest-planned overpass in the US.

Geography

Brooklyn has its lone land border with Queens to the northeast and is situated at the westernmost tip of Long Island. Newtown Creek, which empties into the East River, forms the westernmost portion of this border.

Diverse bodies of water are visible from Brooklyn's shoreline. The East River defines the coastline of northern Brooklyn, while New York Bay borders central Brooklyn. The Red Hook Peninsula and the Erie Basin may be seen from this riverfront section. Buttermilk Channel separates Governors Island from this portion of the beach. The Gowanus Canal connects Gowanus Bay to the southwest. The Narrows, where Upper and Lower New York Bay meet, divides Brooklyn from Staten Island at its farthest southwestern point.

The peninsula on which Coney Island, Brighton Beach, and Manhattan Beach are located is on Brooklyn's southern shore. Jamaica Bay, which is full of islands, borders the southeast coast.

Brooklyn's highest point is at Prospect Park and Green-Wood Cemetery, with an elevation of 200 feet (60 meters) above sea level. Downtown has a little height as well.

Culture

Modern-day Brooklyn is a center of culture. The neighborhood draws artists of various genres looking for inspiration from other artists and the close proximity to Manhattan. Brooklyn draws visitors due to its multicultural character and abundance of activities.

The New York Aquarium and historic Coney Island, the birthplace of Nathan's Hot Dogs and the first amusement park, are close to Brooklyn's South Shore. Shopping is another well-liked activity in this area, where a wide variety of shops provide new and used things, meals and specialized items imported from abroad, vintage and used goods, and just about everything else you can

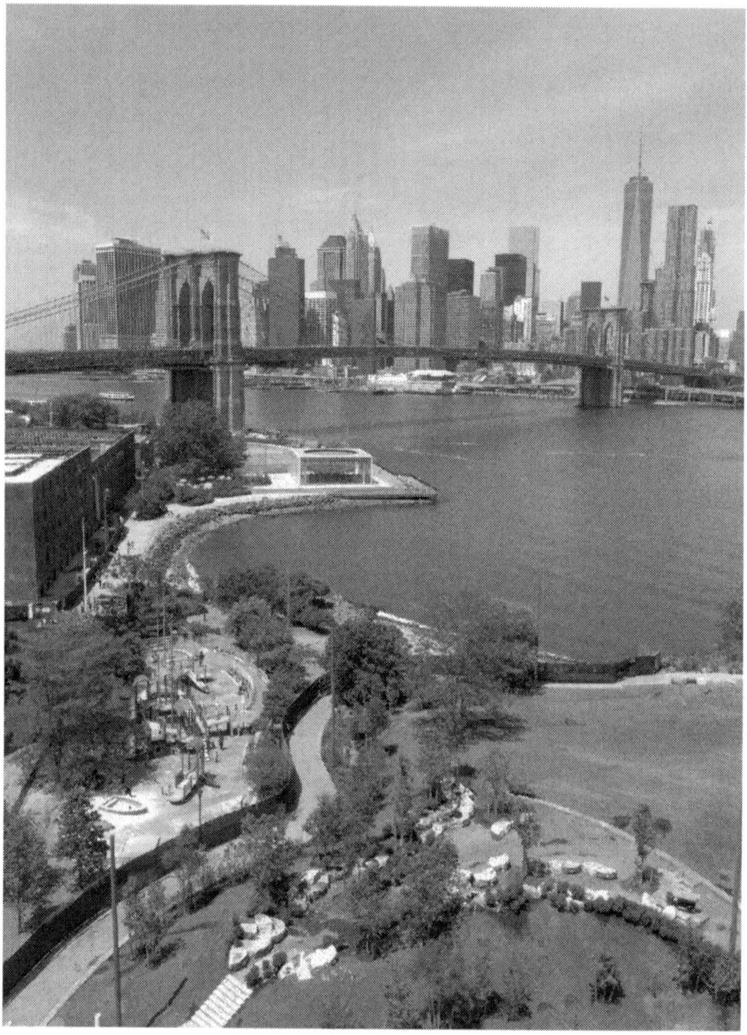

Chapter Two: Planning your trip

Why visit Brooklyn

One of New York City's five boroughs, Brooklyn, has a dynamic and varied culture, making it a great destination. The following are some reasons for thinking about visiting Brooklyn:

Brooklyn is recognized for its multicultural neighborhoods, each with a distinct culture and tradition. Visit Williamsburg, DUMBO, Park Slope, and Bushwick to discover a fusion of different races, cuisines, and creative styles.

Brooklyn boasts a flourishing arts and music scene with various galleries, street art installations, and live music venues. Visit the Brooklyn Museum, which has a sizable collection of artwork from several cultures and eras. Additionally, there are many live music events, particularly in Williamsburg and Bushwick.

Brooklyn is renowned for its young and fashionable districts, which provide a special fusion of innovation and urban charm. Trendy stores, cafés, and bars may be found in neighborhoods like DUMBO and Williamsburg. They are excellent locations to visit and take in the local culture.

Brooklyn has several lovely parks where you can unwind and enjoy the scenery. The same landscape architects who created Central Park also created Prospect Park, which has beautiful green areas, a lake, a zoo, and many recreational opportunities. Brooklyn Bridge Park offers recreational amenities, walking routes, waterfront activities, and breathtaking views of the Manhattan skyline.

Brooklyn is a gastronomic paradise with various international cuisines. You may find food to suit every taste, from chic farm-to-table establishments to classic New York-style pizzerias. The bustling culinary scenes in areas like Park Slope and Williamsburg are especially well-known.

Brooklyn is home to several famous sites that are well worth seeing. A work of technical genius, the Brooklyn Bridge connects Brooklyn and Manhattan and provides stunning vistas. Coney Island is a well-known Brooklyn location ideal for a fun-filled day of sightseeing because of its old amusement park and boardwalk.

Brooklyn has a strong feeling of community, evident in its small shops, farmers' markets, and neighborhood gatherings. Attending street fairs, festivals, and cultural events that highlight the brilliance and creativity of the neighborhood will allow you to feel this vibrant sense of community.

Best Time to Visit Brooklyn

Your selections for weather, events, and activities will determine the ideal time to visit (Brooklyn) New York City. Spring (April to June) and autumn (September to November) are often the busiest travel seasons due to the nice weather, cultural events, and outdoor activities.

With pleasant springtime temperatures in the 50s to 70s Fahrenheit (10 to 21 Celsius), the city springs to life with flowering trees and blooming shrubs. Events like the Tribeca Film Festival and the Brooklyn Botanic Garden's Cherry Blossom Festival occur during this season.

Fall is another fantastic season with pleasant temperatures ranging from the 50s to the 70s Fahrenheit (10 to 21 Celsius). This time of year is incredibly alluring because of the changing hues of the leaves in Central Park and the thrill of occasions like the New York Film Festival and the New York City Marathon.

Although the winter season (December to February) might be chilly and snowy, it can also be a lovely time to travel because of the holiday decorations, ice skating rinks, and the well-known Times Square New Year's Eve celebration. Remember that over the holidays, hotel rates could go up.

New York City's summer, which lasts from June through August, may be hot and muggy, with highs of 70 to 90 degrees Fahrenheit (21 to 32 degrees Celsius). But it's also a period when many outdoor events and activities occur, including outdoor musical performances, Shakespeare in the Park, and several culinary festivals. At major destinations during this time, expect more crowds.

Weather: The greatest seasons for moderate weather are spring (April to June) and autumn (September to November) when daytime highs range from the 50s to the

70s Fahrenheit (10 to 21 Celsius). These times of year provide pleasant weather for outdoor recreation and tourism.

Getting to Brooklyn

Three international airports, which are significant hubs and get traffic from all continents, serve New York City. JFK International Airport (JFK) is the primary airport, followed closely by La Guardia (LGA) and Newark Liberty Airport (EWR), all of which are in New Jersey. The nearest airports to Brooklyn are JFK and LGA.

If you land at Newark Liberty Airport, traveling to Brooklyn (around 40 minutes, depending on traffic) will take longer since you'll have to traverse Manhattan and maybe Queens.

You may travel to Brooklyn via various transportation methods from these airports. Rental cars, buses, the AirTrain (which connects to Subway Line E at Jamaica Station), personal drivers, on-demand transportation, and neighborhood taxis are all options.

Getting To Brooklyn by Car

Every significant national highway in the region is linked to NYC, giving it a natural choice from any surrounding city. Route 95 links to this road from the east at New Haven and the west at Philadelphia, Baltimore, Washington, D.C. Route 76 to Boston, and Route 95 to Pittsburgh. Route 97 travels directly north to Montreal, Canada.

Getting To Brooklyn by Bus

The main stop for buses coming into New York from outside cities is Pennsylvania Station or Port Authority Bus Station. Several well-known companies run routes to New York City, including Bolt bus, Megabus, Peter Pan, and Greyhound.

You may go to Brooklyn from Port Authority Bus Station by taking the DC Brooklyn bus to Empire Blvd. or the subway line Q toward Parkside Av.

Chapter Three:
Neighborhoods of Brooklyn

Williamsburg

One of Brooklyn's most creative districts, Williamsburg, blends old and modern. However, certain aspects of this hipster neighborhood are ageless. Explore the vibrant local arts, music, and boutique scene, write the next great American book on your laptop at several coffee shops, eat at several top-notch restaurants, and take in the vibrant, young vibe.

Old industrial structures, modest attached houses (albeit dotted with a rising number of expensive waterfront high-rises), and a long-standing residential Jewish population serve as the background for the neighborhood's chic atmosphere. If there is one area in Brooklyn that best represents the "new Brooklyn," it is Williamsburg. Williamsburg might sometimes seem alien even if you have lived in Brooklyn for a thousand years. Here are some things to put on your list if you want to explore this fascinating area on your next vacation to New York City.

Things to Do In Williamsburg, Brooklyn

Stroll Through Domino Park

In 2018, the most current Williamsburg activity and addition to the city's offerings were made available to the general public. The old Domino Sugar Refinery, located just north of the Williamsburg Bridge, has been transformed into a 5-acre public park with various amenities.

The park offers beach volleyball, a playground, a taco stand, a fountain, stairs for sitting, and excellent views of the Manhattan skyline from the East River along the Williamsburg shoreline.

The park's name is derived from the location's old sugar refinery. The park's designers, who also built the High-Line in Chelsea, purposely kept some old manufacturing machinery to honour the area's heritage, so you can still see remnants of the past here.

Domino Park is also dog-friendly if you're travelling to Williamsburg with a dog! Or, if you'd rather dine while enjoying a vista, this is among the nicest picnic areas in Brooklyn.

Plan Some Time to Visit Brooklyn Bowl

Suppose you're searching for things to do in Williamsburg. In that case, Brooklyn Bowl is a great choice since it offers a unique spin on your typical bowling alley by combining a music venue with a conventional bowling alley and bar. Even Rolling Stone called it "one of the most incredible places on earth."

A terrific place to have fun is usually the Brooklyn Bowl. Sixteen lanes, a restaurant, and a concert hall are all under one roof. Brooklyn Bowl has established a reputation for itself and has hosted excellent musical events. It is a fun spot to hang out, as previously stated, thanks to coverage from Rolling Stone.

With advice on how to enjoy this popular sight to the fullest, our guide to Williamsburg, Brooklyn, is complete. Plan and check their website for a list of forthcoming events to plan or avoid the busiest times to enjoy this experience. The Brooklyn Bowl gets rather crowded on the weekends, and lanes are first come, first served, so be sure to do so.

On Wythe Avenue, Brooklyn Bowl is conveniently placed in the heart of the nightlife and is open practically all the time. You'll surely have a blast with live music, delicious food, and wonderful company.

For Some Pints And Pins, Go To Gutter Bar!

You'll like this if you enjoyed the previous activity in Williamsburg, Brooklyn. You could choose to bowl if you want to avoid the crowds at concerts or loud music.

Head over to the vintage bowling lanes at Gutter Bar for extra fun if you're looking for a more leisurely game of bowling with a still-enhanced experience complete with beverages, board games, and bar food.

With hardwood flooring and American craft beer, it is referred to be an old-fashioned bowling alley and will make you feel at home.

The 8-lane, sparsely populated alley is ideal for a relaxed weekend or workday.

The gutter bar requires a minimum age of 21 to enter at all hours. So, if you're searching for family-friendly activities in Williamsburg, Brooklyn, check one of our other suggestions instead!

Game Room and Bar At Barcade

Barcade, a pub and arcade, is another of Williamsburg's top nightlife and entertainment options. A few places are scattered across the city, and we are fortunate to have one in Williamsburg.

This fun hangout place offers a full-service bar with excellent beers on tap, an astounding collection of ancient video games, including Pac-Man, Q*bert, and pretty much anything else you can imagine, and an assortment of antique pinball machines.

Grab some tokens and move your drink around as you compete to get the most points.

The City Reliquary Museum Will Let You Discover NYC's Past

Are you interested in history? If so, Williamsburg, Brooklyn, has the activities you're looking for! A truly hidden treasure in Williamsburg, the City Reliquary Museum is a community-run institution that educates visitors about the history of New York City.

This museum is ideal for individuals who want to learn more about artifacts, community collections, and cultural events from both the past and present. If learning something new is on your list of things to do in Williamsburg, it's worth checking out.

Founded by Dave Herman in 2002, this nonprofit museum started as a window exhibit.

The museum features a permanent collection that includes architectural parts from notable buildings, old postcards from local landmarks like The Statue of Liberty, ancient subway tokens, paint chips from the platform of the L train, and other relics from all across the city.

Williamsburg's City Reliquary Museum is open every Thursday through Sunday from noon to six o'clock and is situated at 370 Metropolitan Avenue.

Check out some more incredible Brooklyn museums that are well worth visiting!

McCarren Park

McCarren Park, which shares a boundary with the Green point neighborhood, is another of the greatest outdoor activities in Williamsburg, Brooklyn.

Thirty-five acres of outdoor space are available at McCarren Park. In our Williamsburg, Brooklyn tour, McCarren Park is the ideal place to hang out like a local, even if it is less well-known than the other prominent parks in Brooklyn.

Their baseball diamonds, basketball courts, and grilling areas are perfect for pick-up games, family get-togethers, and friend gatherings. Visit their free outdoor pools if you're searching for somewhere to cool yourself on a hot day!

The Renegade Craft Fair, Movies Under the Stars, and Skill Acquisition workshops are among the enjoyable events offered here throughout the warmer months.

Marsha P Johnson Park

Along the Brooklyn side of the East River, Marsha P Johnson Park offers breathtaking views of Manhattan and the Manhattan skyline. The park is named after Marsha P Johnson, a transgender woman of color who pioneered the LGBTQ civil rights movement and a key figure in the Stonewall Uprising of 1969.

This park is ideal for lounging and relaxing due to its abundant vegetation. A food market held here throughout the summer is now known as Smorgasbord.

Just be aware that bicycles are not permitted here, in contrast to other parks in the city. Although Marsha P Johnson Park welcomes dogs, just two dogs may be brought in at once, just in case you're taking a huge pack of canines.

Bushwick Inlet Park

Another park is yet another of Williamsburg, Brooklyn's greatest outdoor activities. The Williamsburg Waterfront's heart is where Bushwick Inlet Park is situated. This lovely public park, which will extend into the Greenpoint neighborhood, is situated along the East River.

This location is ideal for eating because of the wonderful views.

The park was originally intended to preserve the southbound walkway and gradually add additional layouts towards the north. This park gives Williamsburg a fantastic new appearance. It offers extra green space to the once industrial district, changing it into a welcoming destination for families with excellent city skyline views!

The park is sustainable, which is even better! Here, solar panels, geothermal heating, and a green roof provide the community centre with sustainable energy and warmth.

Cross the Williamsburg Bridge on foot or by bicycle.

The Williamsburg Bridge, which opened in 1903 and was formerly the longest suspension bridge in the world, played a significant part in the history of New York City, even though it may not be as well-known or as gorgeous as the Brooklyn Bridge. There are bike and pedestrian lanes (cyclists should use caution when re-entering Manhattan's traffic), and it's a pleasant substitute for the often congested Brooklyn Bridge.

Green point

Many associate Greenpoint with eccentric, hipster locals who meander with their dogs in strollers and wear knit caps in the summer. While such people are undoubtedly still there, the area is a vibrant hub of culture, cuisine, and entertainment.

Greenpoint is an excellent location for fantastic views since it borders Long Island City to the north and Williamsburg to the south. One must go to the East River to view Brooklyn, Manhattan, and Queens' skylines in all their splendor. Even though the neighborhood seems to be near these places, getting there may be challenging, which is one reason the people of Greenpoint have reclaimed the home as their own.

Things to Do In Greenpoint

At The Józef Pilsudski Institute Of America, Study Local History.

The Józef Pilsudski Institute of America was founded in 1943 to pay tribute to the Polish leader. It functions as a repository, a museum, and a venue for studying contemporary Polish history. You'll learn about important Polish historical occurrences and the accomplishments of Americans of Polish origin.

Visit the archives area to see vintage prints, videos, and photos. You could discover an intriguing book to purchase in the bookshop by browsing ancient and new books on Polish culture and history.

View the extensive permanent collection of fascinating mementoes, historical objects, and artworks by Polish artists. The Ziuk movie theatre also offers the chance to see seminars, exhibits, or feature films.

Visit the Josef Pilsudski Institute of America in the afternoon.

View Modern Art at the Faurschou Foundation

The Faurschou Foundation was established in 2011 by Jens Faurschou, an art collector living in Copenhagen, and his ex-wife Luisa. It exhibits modern artwork from throughout the world. See distinctive exhibits from Eastern and Western cities such as Beijing, Copenhagen, and Venice.

Check out inspiring pieces like "A Boat With Dreams" by Cai Guo-Qiang and "Two Figures" by Ai Weiwei. Visit the skylit gallery to see a variety of artistic mediums, including works like "The Ozymandias Parade" by Edward and Nancy Reddin Kienholz.

Visit the Faurschou Foundation to see other themed and solo shows that showcase partnerships between galleries and artists.

Visit WNYC Transmitter Park to see the sunset

A public park called WNYC Transmitter Park may be found where Greenpoint's Avenue and the banks of the East River meet.

The six-acre site was purchased by WNYC, a public radio station, in 1935.They used the location to transmit an AM signal until it stopped operating in 1990.After that, the city transformed the space into a park, which became accessible to the public in 2012.

The former transmitter building of WNYC is still standing today. Despite being the smallest of Greenpoint's major parks, it offers breathtaking city vistas, particularly around dusk.

Enjoy the Manhattan skyline or take pictures with the massive mural of a girl holding flowers as the backdrop.

Likewise, let your children enjoy themselves on the playground.

Experience a Calming Walk on the Greenpoint's Landing Esplanade

Everyone appreciates the public waterfront space at Greenpoint's Landing Esplanade. It is a part of the Greenpoint's Landing project by the Park Tower Group.

The seaside promenade, grass, and picnic spaces are all part of the 1.5-acre park between the Blue Slip and Bell Slip walkways. Take a stroll while seeing the bustling Manhattan and Long Island. At the picnic tables, spend the day with a snack or coffee.

The sitting area's view of lush vegetation and little trees will make you want to while away the hours.

Visit the Greenpoint Landing Esplanade and have fun.

Visit Monsignor McGolrick Park for Some Solitude

If you're looking for a park with a more laid-back atmosphere, Monsignor McGolrick Park is a great choice.

Monsignor Edward J. McGolrick was a parish leader who assisted in the construction of various institutions in the area. The city dedicated the park in his honour in 1941.

One of the three major parks in the region provides a quiet, discreet location that is dog-friendly and well-shaded with rows of ancient, tall trees. The USS Monitor Building, the memorials honouring the heroes of World War I, and the historic pavilion from 1910 are all nearby.

Little ones may enjoy the swings, play structures, and spray showers in a secured play area with plenty of seating.

Visit Dusty Rose Vintage for shopping

Look for amazing treasures at the enormous warehouse known as Dusty Rose Vintage. Greenpoint's best-kept retail secret is accessible to the general public from Thursday through Sunday and carries anything from antique neckties to grungy denim coats. Dusty Rose Vintage aims to brighten up your wardrobe and social life by offering a range of eccentric, artistic activities like tarot card readings and sketching classes.

WORD Has New Paperback Titles

WORD is one of the most well-liked, small-scale places in Greenpoint. It combines the functions of a community centre with an independent bookstore. WORD has a carefully chosen collection of classic and modern literature and a comprehensive schedule of author readings, seminars, and parties with a literary focus. The staff will take you to the finest book you've never heard of if you let them know what genre you like.

Beer-Swilling At Spritzenhaus 33

Local beer garden Spritzenhaus combines your love of draft beer, German-inspired cuisine, and board games and is great for group trips. Snack on sausages and soft pretzels while perusing the bar's vast beer menu at reasonable prices, then challenge your companions to a tense game of

Jenga. There's no need to make reservations in advance since there's room for everyone.

Visit New Love City and Take a Yoga Lesson

This spacious, cosy yoga studio is in a potted plant-filled Brooklyn apartment. A diverse group of teachers leads daily yoga courses ranging from slow flow for beginners to vinyasa, focusing on fitness. The studio also offers yin and meditation programs in a welcoming setting for individuals who wish to further their practice. Bonus: the G train is only a two-minute walk away.

Visit A Film Noir Theatre To See A Rare Film.

The area has old-fashioned air, and renting a movie fits the bill well. Film Noir, a landmark in Greenpoint owned by Poles and Americans, is a combination video shop and movie theatre. The corner theatre rents out ancient, rare, and independent movies and regularly hosts small screenings (for a few dozen people). Any film enthusiast would get fixated.

122 Meserole Avenue, Brooklyn, New York 11222

Enjoy Some Indie Art.

To appreciate independent art, browse the Brooklyn galleries and visit The Greenpoint Gallery. This nonprofit gallery was established by artist, musician, and visionary Shawn James to foster creativity across all fields by giving New York City artists a convenient and cheap venue for performances, exhibitions, and music rehearsals. Various studio spaces are available for visiting artists, and two levels of roomy galleries. On the website of the gallery, you may

Bushwick

Bushwick, a neighborhood in northern Brooklyn, gets its name from the Dutch phrase "Bushwick," which translates to "little town in words." It borders the Queens neighborhood of Rosewood and the Brooklyn communities of East Williamsburg and Bed-Stuy.

The Canarsie Indians originally inhabited it. Dutch immigrants obtained the area via a deed from the Dutch West India Company, and Governor Peter Stuyvesant incorporated it as one of six Dutch towns in Brooklyn in 1660. Later, the newly arrived British included Bushwick in their Kings County.

After the American Revolutionary War, Bushwick was included in the city of Brooklyn in 1855. It eventually transformed into a borough, and in 1898 it was combined with the rest of Brooklyn to become the City of Greater New York.

Bushwick As It Is Now

Originally farmland, Bushwick transformed into an industrial center in the 19th century. Later, these industrial structures would be transformed into street art canvases or used as dining establishments, studios, and other uses.

The brewing business in Bushwick was established by a wave of German immigrants who arrived in the 1840s and used their brewing expertise in their new country. It would create the "Brewers Row" brewing district. The Ulmer Brewery complex's office building still stands at 31 Belvidere Street between Beaver Street and Broadway.

Bushwick would continue to prosper throughout the 20th century because of the wealth of its residents, but by the 1970s, as manufacturers began to shut, the area had become unpleasant. It was also severely impacted by the 1977 Blackout. By the early 2000s, however, things had changed, and the region was now open to new companies, inhabitants, and visitors like you who could understand why it was so well-liked.

Later, numerous African Americans and immigrants, especially individuals of Irish, Italian, and Jamaican ancestry, would also settle in Bushwick. Today, the area has a sizable Latino population, young urban professionals, and artists. While in New York, are you looking for a multicultural place to visit? Bushwick will appeal to you.

Things to Do In Bushwick

Murals and the Arts Scene in Bushwick

You're in an outdoor museum while walking through Bushwick. Businesses housed in old garages and warehouses have street murals adorning their walls, shutters, pavement, fences, and more. You can see the artist's name in addition to admiring the mural's style and appearance.

For instance, in 2019, artist Chris Stain made edits to "Boy on a Bike," which features a young guy wearing a red cap and a yellow T-shirt. Popular song DFace's hit song "Till Death Do Us Part." It is reported to have drawn inspiration from the illustrations of American pop artist Roy

Lichtenstein and features male and female skeleton heads confronting one another.

Street Art in Bushwick

The Bushwick Collective established by Bushwick resident Joe Ficalora in memory of his late parents and to revitalize the area via the arts, works with local and international artists to paint murals across Bushwick. Additionally, it has a yearly block celebration in June that attracts residents and tourists who like art.

There is a significant amount of street art and many restaurants in the neighborhood around the Bushwick Collective, situated along Troutman Street.

House of Yes

The House of Yes is a cutting-edge performance space and dance club with a nightlife that promotes inclusivity and creativity via events and courses. Their all-night dance events may make you feel like you've entered a fantastical realm.

Scheduled performances at House of Yes may be enthralling to see or listen to, from burlesque performers to aerialists and dance parties. Their venue has hosted a variety of acts throughout the years, including DJs David Morales and Eli Escobar, provocative cabaret actress Susanne Bartsch, and many more.

Restaurants in Bushwick

Bush wick's eating scene has various foods that reflect many cultures and satisfy a range of palates. There are a ton of choices.

Here are a few of my favorites:

Long a mainstay in Bushwick, Roberta's Pizza is renowned for its creative Neapolitan-style and wood-oven baked pies, such as the Bee Sting, made with chile and honey.

Oysters, grilled fish, and seafood are the focus of Sea Wolf, a restaurant with a surf-culture theme. Additionally, it offers a fantastic happy hour daily with specials like $1 wings and oysters and a discount on its signature drink, the Painkiller.

Thai, ramen, and Japanese food are all available at Dock Asian Eatery under one roof. Murals are now being painted on the building's external walls.

You may choose your beyaynetu (a combination of foods with injera flatbread) or order plate's à la carte at the plant-based Ethiopian restaurant Bunna Cafe.

Some of the most excellent tortillas in the area are made on-site at Tortilleria Mexicana Los Hermanos.

The mother-daughter team of Rachel and Catherine Allswang manages Le Garage. It serves French-inspired foods made with Catherine's recipes and is decorated with Rachel's expertise in interior design.

Bushwick Also Has You Covered For Beverages

If you're looking for caffeine, Bushwick boasts an excellent assortment of coffee shops, including Sey Coffee, Little Skips East, and Dweebs. (Mixtape Bushwick also makes creative and mouthwatering breakfast sandwiches to start your day.)

In the morning, Bushwick Public House distributes coffee beverages, and in the evening, it offers house cocktails. The Kings County Brewers Collective, often known as KCBC, which operates a brewery and taproom, claims to be the area's first brewery in forty years.

Shopping In Bushwick

In Bushwick, various alternatives exist for vintage goods, like L Train Vintage and 28 Scott Vintage. A vintage store, an event venue, and a gallery are located within The GG's Social Trade & Treasure Club. Designer clothing, accessories, footwear, and jewelry may be purchased at Chess and the Sphinx.

A second hand bookstore and coffee shop called Molasses Books have a small bar area where customers can read books while obtaining a drink or coffee. Catland Books sells crystals, tarot cards, and other similar things in this multireligious area. Currently, they also provide online tarot readings and other consulting services.

If you like listening to CDs, Vinyl Fantasy offers independent comic books, metal, punk, and experimental music recordings.

Friends is an independent store founded by two friends that sell goods created in Brooklyn apparel, home goods, jewelry, and health items. It is housed at the BogArt, a former warehouse transformed into a studio for artistic output.

Better than Jam's STORE & STUDIO is a textile-related teaching facility that doubles as a store.

FINE & RAW Chocolate, a candy store and espresso bar with a factory in Bushwick that produces delicacies using raw ingredients, is a treat for candy lovers. Pick up their sauce au chocolate et au noix.

Nightlife in Bushwick

Bars, clubs, and other late-night hangouts may be found in Bushwick, even in the last hours of the evening. With astrology-themed drinks and retro lighting, Mood Ring plays on a cosmic concept.

As a cocktail bar and club with science fiction influences, Jupiter Disco also boasts a distinct vibe.

The Pine Box Rock Shop is located within a former casket factory and offers beer, beverages, and sometimes comedic acts.

The Cobra Club makes strangely named cocktails and plans a variety of live performances.

Syndicated combines a bar, a cinema, and a restaurant. You may order food while watching a movie that is being played outside.

Park Slope

Park Slope has a calm, laid-back atmosphere that is almost suburban. On the sidewalks, you'll often see strollers, kids of all ages, people shopping at neighborhood stores, and people walking their dogs to the park. Residents tend to be socially concerned, artistically inclined, and dedicated to their neighborhood since they are true Brooklynites. An informal restaurant atmosphere comes to life at night. Don't search for dancing clubs if you're looking for a night out;

there are many beer gardens and wine bars to visit, particularly on the South Slope.

A natural forest eventually transformed into Prospect Park, one of Brooklyn's most excellent parks, surrounds Park Slope, one of the communities in Brooklyn, New York.

But it wasn't only that that attracted my attention; Park Slope has a rich history throughout the neighborhood, including in the old brown townhouses, museums, halls, and many other places.

Park Slope is the ideal area to find greenery, history, culture, and modernity all in one location.

Where is Park Slope, Brooklyn?

The neighborhood of Park Slope is located in Brooklyn, New York's northwest. The Fourth Avenue and the Prospect Expressway can be reached from the east, while Flatbush Avenue can be reached from the north.

Prospect Park, which gave Park Slope its name, encircles it from the west to the east.

Things to Do In Park Slope

Explore Prospect Park

Prospect Park, which was created by the same architects as Central Park, is the name of the neighborhood. There is something for everyone there, including a dog beach, a music pavilion, and a zoo. When I'm not simply wondering about, however, I go with friends for an unplanned weekend picnic. We have a site we call "the spot" so we can meet up in the vast meadows.

Visit BAM to See a Performance.

Strange theater and dance, book presentations, and the odd live podcast session are all things I like. All of these are offered abundantly by BAM.

Go Spot Patrick Stewart

Following his infamous purchase of a Brownstone close to the park a few years ago, Patrick Stewart is now often seen by neighborhood residents visiting coffee shops or the Park Slope Food Co-op.

Drink Craft Beer at Uncle Barry's

The modest garden of Uncle Barry's (A Bar) is ideal for catching up with friends on a Saturday afternoon before an event at the Barclay's Center and has a changing a variety of US-made artisan beers from different states.

Stuff Yourself At Dinosaur Bar-B-Que.

The meal they term "BBQ" in New York has often let me down as a Kansas City native, but Dinosaur Barbeque has restored my trust in the dish. The brisket is no joke, and the pulled pork makes me so happy even though it's not KC BBQ.

Tapas and cocktails are available at Blueprint.

When I want to catch up with a buddy I haven't seen in a long, I turn to Blueprint. A fantastic conversational evening is made possible by fancy drinks, a sizable wine selection, and amazing charcuterie platters. There is also a backyard!

Get Fancy at Al Di La

The go-to place for really outstanding Italian cuisine and wine is this local oratorio, which has been around for a very long time.

Records may be found at Music Matters.

Despite the shop's small size, the collection is extensive. The owner, who works the register, will order it in time for your brother-in-law's birthday if they don't have it in stock (not that I would know).

Coffee at the Hungry Ghost

In BK, great coffee is simple to get by, yet something about the Hungry Ghost's eerie atmosphere keeps me returning. A further benefit of the "no laptops allowed" regulation is that it prevents campers from occupying the coveted seats.

Visit the Old Stone House to learn more about the Battle of Brooklyn.

A museum on the Battle of Brooklyn in 1776 has been established on the ground floor of the building with the same name. I used to spend all my time at the nearby park until I discovered the museum after hearing the Hamilton score a few (hundred) times.

BKLYN Larder Offers Cheesy Cuisine

They provide breakfast sandwiches, cured meats, and expensive cheese. Is the fancy cheese mentioned?

Eat Some Bagels at the Pub

Because the bagels at Bagel Pub are a notch above the rest, my cousin often requires that I meet her a few blocks from either of our homes. My preferred sandwich is toasted pumpernickel with scallion cream cheese, although I've also heard that anything with lox is wonderful.

Visit Dizzy's For Brunch

Dizzy's is a very traditional corner diner, but the cuisine is AMAZING. If you don't there early, you may have to choose from among the other 800 mouthwatering brunch spots since it fills up quickly. as Miriam. also alchemy.

Visit the Chocolate Room to Satisfy Your Sweet Tooth

The Chocolate Room, a popular among those searching for things to do in Park Slope at night, is a traditional post-dinner destination for many first dates. But in my opinion, it's fantastic whether you need a fast pick-me-up, a chocolate cocktail, or to restock your home supply.

Brooklyn's Very Own Park

The area's green oasis and beating heart is Prospect Park, Brooklyn's version of Central Park, which was opened in 1867. After finishing work on Central Park in Manhattan, Frederick Law Olmsted and Calvert Vaux created the 2.4 square kilometer park. Visit this landmark if you're seeking for things to do in Park Slope. Along with several sizable green spaces, like Long Meadow, the park also offers a number of unique features. On 24 acres of land in Prospect Park, there is just one lake in Brooklyn. The Litchfield Villa, once the residence of Edwin Clark Litchfield, serves as the Brooklyn headquarters for the New York City Department of Parks and Recreation.

The Prospect Park Zoo, a boathouse, the Botanical Gardens, the Prospect Park Band shell (a concert venue), and other sports entertainment venues (such as a baseball field, tennis center, basketball courts, and soccer fields) are among the park's additional attractions. Prospect Park is a great retreat during the warmer months, much like Central Park. The park is regarded by locals as the neighborhood's greatest asset.

There are over 200 different types of birds living in the park, which many people find amazing if you want to observe birds.

Grand Army Plaza: Prospect Park's Main Entrance

We advise using the main entrance when you enter the park. The Grand Army Plaza serves as Prospect Park's main entrance. The Grand Army Plaza is situated at the confluence of Flatbush Avenue, Eastern Parkway, and Prospect Park West in Brooklyn.

A memorial of immense significance to the city of New York City is the Arc de Triumphed in New York, a replica of one of France's most significant structures. Between 1861 and 1865, the Soldiers 'and Sailors' Arch, a charming archway honoring the Union's defenders, served as the centerpiece of Grand Army Plaza.

In the same vicinity lies the Brooklyn Public Library, which is also well worth a visit

Brooklyn Botanic Garden Prospect Park

The Brooklyn Botanic Garden is yet another of Park Slope's most well-liked attractions. It is the city's natural marvel and a big draw during cherry blossom season. Many people go directly to Brooklyn's Botanic Garden to see this natural show. For more details about cherry blossoms, go here.

There are several distinct separate gardens spread across the garden. The Cranford-Rosengarten's aroma will linger in your memory for days, the Japanese hill-pond garden emanates calmness and peace, and the Steinhardt conservatory, home to the renowned CV Starr Bonsai Museum, beckons you inside for a walk. Brooklyn Botanic Garden entrance is free for holders of New York Passes.

Sporting Events at the Barclays Center

Sports events are among the top things to do in Park Slope. The Barclays Center, the newest arena in New York City, sits just on the boundary of Park Slope, thus it's not quite within the neighborhood. This arena serves as the Brooklyn Nets' new home and serves as their fourth team name. The New Jersey Americans, The New York Nets, and finally The New Jersey Nets were their original names.

The basketball team has been referred to as the Brooklyn Nets since 2012. Music entrepreneur Jay-Z contributed to the Nets' relocation to Brooklyn.

Despite the initial mistrust of Brooklyn locals, the relocation and building of the stadium are part of a plan to bring Downtown Brooklyn back to its previous splendor.

On our website, it's simple to get Brooklyn Nets tickets in advance. The lowest priced ticket is $28. For your information, the NBA season lasts from October to April. NHL games and even boxing may be seen. On the East Coast, the Barclays Center has emerged as the center of boxing.

Brooklyn Museum

The Brooklyn Museum is among the most well-liked activities in Park Slope. It serves as Brooklyn's equivalent of the Metropolitan Museum of Art in Manhattan. The museum, designed in 1897 by McKim, Mead, and White, includes more over 2 million works of art, ranking it eighth among US institutions.

Both the pre-Columbian collection and the Egyptian collection have exhibitions, which are both located on the first and fourth floors, respectively. More than 20 living and dining rooms from New England mansions built between 1675 and 1830 are on exhibit in the so-called "Period Rooms" on the fifth floor.

Along with receiving a very comprehensive overview of US art, visitors also see Albert Bierstadt's "A storm in the Rocky Mountains" and other pieces. There are usually performances, contentious discussions, and other events at the Museum (address: 200 Eastern Pkwy, Brooklyn), so make sure to check the schedule of activities in advance.

These events include swing dance or portraiture courses, movie screenings, world music concerts, and hip-hop DJ sets.

Brooklyn Heights

Mostly low-rise brick and brownstone row homes with a few apartment buildings, trees, playgrounds, and religious organizations comprise the area. Our primary retail area is Montague Street, but other intriguing shops and eateries are hidden on our small lanes along Henry Street.

Where In New York City Is Brooklyn Heights?

Between Dumbo to the north, Downtown Brooklyn to the east, and Cobble Hill to the south sits Brooklyn Heights.

Atlantic Avenue Subway: A, C, R, W, 2, 3, 4, 5 Cadman Plaza West to the East River East to the Brooklyn Bridge Promenade North to South Boundaries

Brooklyn Bridge, Brooklyn-Queens Expressway, and NYC Ferry services are available for a ticket out of the city.

Things to do in Brooklyn Heights

The majority of things to do and see in Brooklyn Heights are free. We used to do these activities to have fun on the weekends and throughout the week while still living here.

Walk Across the Brooklyn Bridge

Did you know that Brooklyn Heights was Manhattan's first suburb? It is real!

Earlier than the Brooklyn Bridge's construction (it's nearby! Instead, they had to take a boat. Try to walk across, or at least give it a go halfway.

The Brooklyn Bridge is best visited between 7 and 9 in the morning. It's one of the finest free experiences in NYC for tourists and residents alike.

View the Stores on Henry Street and Montague Street

There are just two distinct business sectors in Brooklyn Heights. They are Henry Street near the Clark Street subway station (2 and 3 lines) and Montague Street between Clinton and Hicks.

There are plenty of shops and eateries in each of these locations. The bar and café scene in Brooklyn Heights is a touch underwhelming.

Our favorite restaurant in Brooklyn Heights is Lantern Thai, so if you're hungry, go there. Visit Emack & Bolio's Ice Cream for dessert, without a doubt.

On your way to the park, you may stop at Key Food Supermarket or Fresh Start Marketplace (Montague between Clinton and Court St.) for refreshments. If it's brunch time, dine at Le Pain Quotidien or head to the Heights Cafe and sit outdoors to watch people-watch.

The Brooklyn Cat Cafe, a new cat cafe, has opened on Montague Street. It is located on Montague, a beautiful, peaceful street between Hicks Street and Montague Terrace.

Find the Dead Ends at Love Lane, Hunts Lane, and Grace Court Alley to Learn the Local Secrets

Love Lane, Hunts Lane, and Grace Court Alley are three of Brooklyn's loveliest alleyways and some of the city's tiniest streets. Converted carriage cottages and peaceful doorsteps may be found on these little dead-end alleys. In the area's early days, couples would stroll down Love Lane and go on dates there, thereby earning the street its name.

These lanes are great for snapping a quick snapshot or two. Please be considerate if you take pictures of people's houses in these alleys since they live there and all the residences are private.

Locate the Brownstone With A Concealed Ventilator On Joralemon Street.

The most vibrant hues may be seen on Joralemon Street, which also has a façade that doubles as a ventilation facility for the 4 and 5 metro lines that run under it. Can you locate it?" Most locals aren't familiar with this building. It nearly seems to fit.

Keep your eyes open; else, you could stroll right past. Okay, the location is now public knowledge: 58 Joralemon Street.

Consider Staying at 1Hotel In Brooklyn Heights.

It's not a secret, 1Hotel. There is a brand-new, really hip hotel nearby. If you're out and about in Brooklyn Bridge Park, you may get a snack at the café on the first level, which serves coffee and pastries.

You may take in the gorgeous décor in the foyer of 1 Hotel. A distinctive design, vertical plants hanging from the walls and a magnificent restaurant are all present.

There may sometimes be complimentary fruit, cookies (more cookies!), and beverages near the elevators. Take the elevators up to the top to enjoy the fantastic views of the East River.

Look For the Fruit Streets in Brooklyn Heights

Explore the quaintly designed Fruit Streets, including Orange Street, Cranberry Street, and Pineapple Street. Your mental image of Brooklyn Heights is this place.

Since Henry Street, where more commerce occurs, is where the Fruit Streets branch out from, they are primarily residential. Respecting everyone's privacy is essential since the brownstones and historic houses are all the residences of actual people.

The Wooden Footbridge of the Brooklyn Bridge

At the Promenade's terminus, there is a wooden bridge. You are brought to DUMBO. You may use this shortcut or stroll down the street to arrive at DUMBO.

The bridge's location is not a secret, but we'd love it if it were because it can become hectic. To learn our trick, come here at the end of the day to enjoy the vista.

Look For the Brooklyn Heights Promenade

The Brooklyn Heights Promenade may be reached by either Montague or Remsen Street. You may get to the Promenade's terminus by using these streets.

When the sky begins to change beyond the silhouettes of the Statue of Liberty and the Lower Manhattan Skyline, you should arrive during the golden hour and remain until sunset.

Running, walking the dog, and strolling with friends and family are all enjoyable activities here. It may draw a sizable number of visitors, but early and late, it's only for residents.

Columbia Heights, which is located between Orange and Cranberry Street, is where the Brooklyn Heights Promenade comes to an end.

DUMBO

You will arrive in one of N.Y.C.'s most charming districts, whether you enter DUMBO on foot, via boat, or through the A, C, or F subway lines. The neighborhood known as DUMBO, which stands for Down Under the Manhattan Bridge Overpass, is well-known for its breathtaking views of Manhattan, first-rate waterfront park, thriving art, and food scenes, and what might be N.Y.C.'s most Instagrammable hot spot: the intersection of Washington Street and Water Street with the Manhattan Bridge in the distance.

This section of Brooklyn, however, was sometimes more quaint. The area was formerly an industrial center before becoming a popular tourist destination. The ancient structures, now loft apartments and art galleries, were factories that manufactured everything from cardboard boxes to Brillo pads (both of which were created in DUMBO) during their industrial heyday in the 19th and 20th centuries. A flood of artists poured into the region in the 1970s, spurring developers to take another look at the East River-adjacent neighborhood when manufacturing slowed down during the Depression.

Things to Do In Dumbo

Discover a Thriving Culinary Scene

Pizza is a must-try on any culinary tour of Brooklyn, and DUMBO is home to two New York institutions: Grimaldi's and Juliana's, both of which were established by famed pizza maker Pasquale "Patsy" Grimaldi (the latter of which is still connected to the Grimaldi family). The brunch scene and the pizza wars are highly recognized in the area. For casual American cuisine, visit Westville; for classic diner fare, visit Clark's Restaurant; or for avocado toast, flat whites, and other Australian classics, visit Bluestone Lane. Another hidden treasure is Vinegar Hill House, which serves quiche and pancakes with seasonal twists. Try Kogane Ramen, where the noodles are prepared daily for a non-brunch afternoon meal.

You may also eat takeaway from Bread & Spread, a well-known Italian sandwich shop, or The Migrant Kitchen. This immigrant-run catering business provides Middle Eastern-Latin food while lounging in the sun in Brooklyn Bridge Park. Need some motivation? You can get robust, excellent coffee at the streamlined, minimalist Japanese import Arabica or the La Colombe-brewing Archway Cafe.

There are plenty of sweets in the area, beginning with baked products, for those with a sweet appetite. You may get morning pastries at the more diverse Butler Bakeshop or the French bakery Almondine. For cakes and cookies, visit Burrow for treats with French and Japanese influences or Jacques Torres for his famous chocolate chip cookie. Need something chilly to eat? There are many varieties to pick from since Ample Hills, Oddfellows, Brooklyn Ice Cream Factory, and Sugar Hill Creamery are all close by.

There is a restaurant for every taste when it is time for supper. Enjoy regional Mexican cuisine at Gran Electrica, seasonal French cuisine at Atrium, seafood, and small plates inspired by Saigon at Em Vietnamese (pro tip: try the garlic butter clams). Consider Celestine for wood-fired Mediterranean cuisine and its breathtaking waterfront setting, Osprey for farm-to-table New American cuisine, or The River Café, a Brooklyn landmark and one of N.Y.C.'s most romantic restaurants, with sweeping views of the city skyline and a fine-dining menu.

Find Out More About Craft Beer And Cocktail Culture.

The bars in DUMBO are among the best in the city, even if the bar scene may not compare to other areas. Twenty rotating taps at the newest Evil Twin Brewing location will make beer geeks feel right at home, while Olympia Wine Bar has a great range of reds and whites available by the glass or bottle for wine lovers. Visit Superfine for inexpensive drinks (including a killer bloody Mary) or Almar for traditional cocktails with an Italian twist. In the warmer months, DUMBO Station, the temporary bar located in the Archway, serves beer and wine for outdoor drinking.

Explore the Outdoors, Art, and Shopping.

Even though DUMBO is a tiny area, there is much to see and do there. Its focal point is the enchanting Brooklyn Bridge Park, which stretches for 1.3 miles from Columbia Heights to the Manhattan Bridge and is interesting to explore on its whole length. Construction on the beautiful meadows, playgrounds, sports fields, and meticulously restored Jane's Carousel began more than ten years ago. No matter your age, it would help if you took a spin on the vintage carousel created by award-winning architect Jean Nouvel. From there, you can go to Washington Street, the often Instagrammed cobblestone block of the Manhattan Bridge, framed by two old red brick buildings, and Pebble Beach, which offers unobstructed views of downtown Manhattan.

Though the burgeoning tech area DUMBO may get more attention now, the artists who lived there in the 1970s are credited with giving the neighborhood its name. The site still has a significant gallery presence. On First Thursdays, several studios remain open late, such as the fiber arts experts Loop of the Loom, the women and non-binary-led A.I.R., and Smack Mellon. Some galleries do more than merely present art; Superfine, for example, features a new artist's work each month, while Usagi combines an exhibition space, a bookshop, and a micro-roaster.

There is a ton more activities to keep you occupied. For a more sedate experience, visit the independent publisher Melville House Bookshop or the woman-owned Adanne, which specializes in books by Black writers? You can also browse new releases in the expansive Powerhouse Arena at the Archway. Catch a live performance at Bargemusic, a floating concert hall that performs chamber music while anchored on the East River, or St. Ann's factory, which presents modern plays and concerts within a tobacco factory converted into a theater.

Stay The Night In A Boutique Hotel With Breathtaking Views.

You'll need a spot to retire to after a day of sightseeing. The fashionable 1 Hotel Brooklyn Bridge, close to Pier 1, features a prime location, rooftop bar, spa, plunge pool, and other amenities. The New York Marriott at Brooklyn Bridge is a little further away but offers just as many facilities, including two restaurants offering cuisine from the surrounding area, wine from Brooklyn Winery, and a fitness facility with Peloton cycles.

Red Hook

With its urban feel, Red Hook, Brooklyn captures the very heart of New York City's raw character, making it a sanctuary for artists, musicians, businesspeople, and designers. Red Hook is the perfect location for a day excursion free of busy crowds and hoards of visitors despite its several unfinished construction sites, breathtaking view of the Statue of Liberty, and countless fashionable stores.

With its urban feel, Red Hook, Brooklyn captures the very heart of New York City's raw character, making it a sanctuary for artists, musicians, businesspeople, and designers. Red Hook is the perfect location for a day excursion free of busy crowds and hoards of visitors despite its several unfinished construction sites, breathtaking view of the Statue of Liberty, and countless fashionable stores.

Things to Do In Redhook

Visit the Museum on the Waterfront and Showboat Barge

The Waterfront Museum and Showboat Barge preserve and honor this vital transportation system's splendor from 1860 to 1960 when the waterways were bustling with cargo ships bringing products. Red Hook was formerly one of New York City's largest shipyards. The Lehigh Valley Railroad Barge Number 79, the last of its type still coated in wood, is where the Museum is situated. Visitors are welcome to explore the Museum's intriguing antiquities while it sways back and forth with the tide for free. The barge presents various theatrical and musical productions throughout the year, including tugboat excursions, special exhibits, a showboat circus, river songs, a pirate show, ballet, theater, and opera.

Visit the Basin Of Erie

The 18th to 20th-century jewels and antiquities found in Erie Basin are guaranteed to fascinate all art and history enthusiasts! The interior of Erie Basin is not only visually appealing, with a polished black floor and matte white walls that highlight the extraordinary collection of vintage jewelry, but it also contains a positively dazzling assortment of priceless brooches, rings, earrings, necklaces, and cufflinks that are one-of-a-kind. A tiny mosaic scarab bracelet, the 1870s carved wooden pharaoh, and emerald pharaoh earrings are among the intriguing new Egyptian Revival pieces that Erie Basin has just placed. The Museum also exhibits artifacts from the Georgian, Victorian, Edwardian, Retro and Modern, and Art Deco periods.

See What Baked Offers

With its well-regarded, delectable scones, muffins, cakes, and cookies, Baked raises the bar for culinary and baking prowess. The two master cooks behind the counter have converted their baking aspirations into a wild success by changing their Brooklyn bakery's woodsy ambiance and rustic orange décor into a desert paradise. Oprah and

Martha Stewart have recognized and commended them for their wonderful baked delicacies. The Red Hook Red Hot cupcake, a red velvet confection made with Valrhona cocoa and drizzled with cinnamon buttercream, caramel coconut cluster bars, and The Salted Caramel shortbread, the Red Hook Red Hot cupcake, which is a red velvet treat baked with Valrhona chocolate and covered with cinnamon buttercream. Any visitor or local who visits will be sure to enjoy them.

Get a Sip at Brooklyn Ice House

With a beer menu featuring more than 50 domestic and foreign brews and an excellent selection of bar food, including the cheesy, bacon-loaded Dirty Dog and the signature pulled-pork sandwich served with copious amounts of barbeque sauce and a tangy pickle for a twist of flavor, Brooklyn Ice House has earned its place as a longtime neighborhood favorite. It is the perfect weekend hangout location to talk, laugh, and chat with old friends and strangers, thanks to the red leather banquettes, wood paneling, restroom blackboard wall, and casual, comfy rear patio!

Red Hook Restaurants the Taste You Will Never Forget

Gourmet food vendors appear throughout Brooklyn in the spring, summer, and autumn, yelling and selling their delectable ethnic street food to onlookers. The Red Hook Latin American Food Vendors from El Salvador, Guatemala, Colombia, Mexico, the Dominican Republic, and Puerto Rico often occupy the ball fields. The pupusas (a corn tortilla filled with cheese, zucchini, and pork), (corn on a stick, coated in mayo and chili powder), and tamales, in addition to the well-known and adored packed tacos, burritos, and empanadas, attract audiences from all over the city with their distinctive tastes and spices. These finger appetizers are so delicious when paired with a sweet tamarind beverage or a refreshing watermelon juice that you'll return to the food carts for more within minutes!

Check Out the North Inuit Art Gallery

The Look North Inuit Art Gallery is situated in a recently refurbished Civil War-era building that was originally a shipping warehouse but has since been turned into a refuge of creative expression. It is conveniently located in Red Hook's thriving art scene. Established less than ten years ago, the Inuit art exhibit provides visitors with a stunning waterfront perspective of New York Harbor and the city in the background while showcasing the outstanding artwork of close to 30 Inuit settlements in Canada's Arctic area. Educational tours and exhibits show traditional Inuit stone sculptures, photographic prints, paintings, and etchings, educating New Yorkers about a lesser-known form of artistic expression.

Park and Pier for Louis Valentino Jr

Louis Valentino Jr Park and Pier offer a million-dollar vista of Lady Liberty, Lower Manhattan, Governors Island, Staten Island, and the Red Hook Stores Building from the Civil War in a cove off New York Bay. In addition to the lovely view, Louis Valentino Park has a large area of lush green grass for recreational activities and relaxation, free summertime outdoor movie screenings, and a shoreline next to the pier for canoeing and kayaking (which is accessible on Sunday afternoons and Thursday evenings in the summer). This area once used for shipping, is now a family favorite for picnics, kite flying, and tranquil late-night strolls.

Pioneer Works

An eclectic cultural center called Pioneer Works presents a variety of artwork and an open studio series every second Sunday of the month, as well as free public musical concerts, exhibitions, and other special events. Pioneer Works is a hub for studying and exploring contemporary cultural expression by artists, scientists, theorists, educators, and musicians via on-site residencies in the arts and sciences and educational initiatives. Everybody who wanders in is welcome, and the leading exhibition, artist-in-residence studios, and tours are all free. Hours are Wednesday through Sunday, 12pm to 6pm

77|BROOKLYN TRAVEL GUIDE 2023

Chapter Four: Attractions in Brooklyn

Brooklyn Bridge

Between Manhattan and Brooklyn in New York, a suspension bridge called the Brooklyn Bridge spans the East River. Building a bridge across the East River has been discussed extensively. The strait could only be crossed by boat. Engineer John Augustus Roebling first suggested building a suspension bridge across the channel in 1855, and he was selected to design the bridge in 1869. After 14 years of building, the bridge was finally completed in 1883. During that time, many workers perished, notably John Augustus Roebling.

One of the earliest contemporary suspension bridges, the Brooklyn Bridge, was the first to be built using steel cables. The main span of the 1825-meter-long Brooklyn Bridge is 486 meters. Until the Williamsburg Bridge opened in 1903, the bridge was the most significant suspension bridge in the world. One of the most well-known bridges in the world and a famous icon in New York is the Brooklyn Bridge.

Prospect Park

Prospect Park was created over thirty years (1865–1895) by Frederick Law Olmsted and Calvert Vaux, the architects of Central Park, and has since become a prominent attraction for tourists and Brooklyn residents.

The park is a perfect green area well recognized for its complicated artificial watercourse (wetlands) and its trees, which make up most of Brooklyn's surviving native forest. Its 526 acres are home to a zoo, the country's first urban Audubon Center, an ice rink, a band shell, a carousel, and several sporting and recreational facilities.

Start your excursions immediately and join the eight million tourists who enjoy this lovely park each year.

Events

- Scavenger hunt
- Nature reflection and journaling

Facilities

- Barbecuing Areas
- Baseball Fields
- Bicycling and Greenways
- Dog-friendly Areas
- Eateries
- Fishing
- Fitness Equipment
- Great Trees
- Hiking Trails
- Historic Houses
- Horseback Riding Trails
- Ice Skating Rinks
- Nature Centers
- Playgrounds
- Public Restrooms
- Spray Showers
- Tennis Courts
- Wi-Fi Hotspots
- Zoos and Aquariums

Brooklyn Museum

Brooklyn Museum is a Brooklyn, New York-based museum of art and a leader in art education, community engagement, and service. The museum's first portion was inaugurated in 1897. In 1923, it became the first museum in the United States to display African cast metal and other things as art rather than as ethnological relics after adding wings and specialized facilities throughout the years. In 1929, the first installation of a period chamber was inaugurated. 1955 saw the addition of 12 Assyrian alabaster reliefs to the museum's holdings. One of the best collections of Egyptian art in the world is housed in the museum. There is also a representation of the arts from Asia, Oceania, the Americas, and Africa. Cubism, black American art, women's art, and Haitian art are examples of the various subjects featured in special shows.

Barclays Center

Since its completion on September 28, 2012, the Barclays Center in the heart of Brooklyn has established itself as the premier venue for the world's most exciting sporting and entertainment events. The cutting-edge arena, home to the

NHL's New York Islanders and the NBA's Brooklyn Nets, is a showcase for eco-friendly design and building practices after receiving the U.S. Green Building Congress' LEED® Silver Certification for New Construction.

The 2013 Sports Business Awards Sports Facility of the Year, 2013 Pollstar Arena of the Year, Architizer A+ Building of the Year Award, and Brooklyn Chamber of Commerce Brooklyn Building Award for Economic Development are just a few essential awards that Barclays Center has received. It offers 17,732 basketball fans, 15,795 hockey fans, and up to 19,000 spectators for musical and cultural shows with compact seating options with unrivaled sightlines.

Brooklyn Botanic Garden

The Brooklyn Botanic Garden is a botanical garden located in the Brooklyn neighborhood of New York City. It was constructed in 1910 on land taken from Mount Prospect Park in the heart of Brooklyn, next to Prospect Park and the Brooklyn Museum.

Over 14,000 different plant species may be found in the 52-acre garden, which welcomes over a million people annually. It has many specialty "gardens within the Garden," plant collections, the C. V. Starr Bonsai Museum in the Steinhardt Conservatory, three climate-themed plant pavilions, an art gallery, and an aquatic plant house made of white cast iron and glass.

Brooklyn Flea Market

Brooklyn, New York, is home to the well-known outdoor market, the Brooklyn Flea. It is renowned for its distinctive fusion of handmade and antique products and its wide range of food sellers. The market sells various goods, including collectibles, furniture, apparel, accessories, and antiques.

Beginning in 2008, the Brooklyn Flea Market rapidly established itself as a must-see attraction for residents and visitors. It has expanded in size and appeal, drawing sellers from around the city and beyond.

In Brooklyn's Williamsburg, a hip district, the Brooklyn Flea Market has one of its most well-known venues. The market typically runs on the weekends, allowing visitors to explore and buy one-of-a-kind items in a bustling and dynamic setting.

Various food sellers are available at the market in addition to antique and handcrafted goods. You may choose from many delectable delicacies, including artisanal nibbles and foods from other countries. It's a fantastic location for a quick meal before touring the market.

Before planning travel plans, it's wise to check the Brooklyn Flea's official website or social media channels for the most up-to-date information since market schedules and locations might sometimes change.

Industrial City

A mixed-use building called Industry City may be found in Sunset Park, Brooklyn, New York. A large industrial area has become a bustling location for food, shopping, co working, and events.

Industry City has experienced a considerable revival in recent years. It was first constructed as a manufacturing and storage complex in the early 20th century. Today, it houses a variety of companies, including those that create artisanal food and drinks, retail establishments, art galleries, and creative offices.

There are several facilities and attractions available on the property. Visitors may browse the numerous boutiques and stores, indulge in delectable food and beverages from neighborhood vendors, and see exciting art installations and exhibits. Additionally, Industry City has frequent events, including concerts, fairs, and seminars.

Industry City is home to a developing community of companies and entrepreneurs in addition to its retail and leisure options. The facility offers contemporary office spaces and adaptable co working solutions for startups, independent contractors, and established businesses.

Public transit is convenient for getting to Industry City, with several bus and metro lines servicing the neighborhood. Industry City is located at 220 36th Street, Brooklyn, NY 11232.

.

Chapter Five: Food and Drink in Brooklyn

8 Brooklyn Foods You Must Try Once in Your Life

Pizza from L&B Spumoni Gardens in Bensonhurst

L&B Spumoni Gardens' squares have yet to be consumed. Why are you holding out? L&B is among the top pizzerias in the nation, and that's saying a lot (which is why we take you there on our Pizza Tour). You got it, Sicily, Italy, is where Sicilian-style pizza originated, and L&B offers it. Pies are often square or rectangular with a thicker crust; the sauce is added to the cheese. The traditional L&B "squares" were created when they prepared pizza as their Sicilian grandmother had taught them.

Nathan's Famous Hot Dog from Coney Island

There is such a thing as the ideal hot dog, and you can get it at Nathan's Famous! In 1916, Nathan's started as a one-cent hot dog stand and is still in business today. German Frankfurters made entirely of beef were placed within a long roll that Charles Feldman created at his Park Slope bakery. At 10 cents apiece, he dubbed them "Coney Island Red Hots," and they were a big success. They eventually started going by the name "hot dogs."

At Feltman's restaurant, Nathan Handwerker had a job. Eddie Cantor and Jimmy Durante, the singer and pianist at Feltman's, gave Nathan a $350 loan to start up his hot dog stand near the intersection of Surf and Stillwell Avenues. Nathan made an all-beef hot dog using a recipe from his mother-in-law. Additionally, Cantor and Durante persuaded Nathan to sell his hot dogs for 5 cents apiece instead of 10 cents as Feltman did. Feltman wouldn't lower his pricing to even just a cent. According to urban myth, Feltman's and Nathan's coexisted for over 40 years until Nathan's forced it out of business.

Bagel from Bagel Hole in Park Slope

If you want a real Brooklyn bagel, Bagel Hole in Brooklyn's Park Slope neighborhood is the place to go. They are spicy, crunchy, chewy, and traditional. Because their bagels are smaller than people are accustomed to nowadays, Bagel Hole receives criticism but only maintains the original. Bagels SHOULD be made in that manner. We can all agree that, at least in terms of bagels, Mayor DiBlasio once said that they were the greatest in New York City. ????

Porter House from Peter Luger Steakhouse in Williamsburg

You only truly live if you have Peter Luger Steakhouse's renowned porterhouse steak!

It holds a Michelin Star, has been named the best steakhouse in all of New York by Zagat since 1984, and, most significantly, is highly recommended by Brooklyn residents.

Regarding Their Meat, Peter Luger Is Quite Picky

If desired, the short loins and shells are brought to each restaurant's on-site dry maturing facilities. Here, the temperature, humidity, and airflow are tightly controlled environments where they are stored. The short loins are killed, trimmed, and taken to the kitchen for broiling when suitably aged. A steak at Peter Luger's will be among the best in the nation thanks to their meticulous selection procedure.

Fried Calamari at Sheep Head Bay's Randazzo's Clam Bar

Before eating fried calamari at Randazzo's Clam Bar, you have yet to experience it.

In 1916, Helen Randazzo's founded Randazzo's, which still operates today and offers some of Brooklyn's top seafood dining options. Approach the window and ask for some fried calamari or a dozen half-shelled clams. You'll never lose! Additionally, supporting a company run by a family is always excellent.

Italian Cookies from Carroll Gardens' Court Pastry

Italian cuisine in its purest form is undoubtedly a specialty of Brooklyn, and Court Pastry is no exception. Since 1948, they have been producing classic desserts like biscotti and cannoli. When you enter the family-run business, get ready for sensory overload. You won't believe how wonderful it smells. Court Pastry is more than just a store; it's a landmark.

Sandwich Made with Roast Beef at Sheep head Bay's Roll N Roaster.

When in Brooklyn, a visit to Roll-R-Roaster is a no-brainer. Their roast meat is cooked to your preferences after being gently roasted all day. They thinly slice it, heap it on freshly made buns, and then top it with optional cheese and natural pan gravy.

Junior's On Flatbush Avenue Cheesecake

We've said it before, and we'll repeat it: Junior's cheesecake may be found in the dictionary under "cheesecake." Over the last 50 years, the Flatbush Avenue institution has been serving its delectable, melt-in-your-mouth cheesecake, and the recipe has remained almost unchanged.

Craft Beer and Breweries
Brooklyn Breweries

For many years, Brooklyn has served as a center for craft brewing. Before Prohibition, Brooklyn was the nation's center of brewing, producing more than 10% of the nation's beer! Brooklyn still has a robust beer business today, with several breweries launching each year.

Also held in Brooklyn is the NYC Beer Week Festival. Brewers and beer enthusiasts from near and far alike are looking forward to this event! It simply illustrates how unique the craft beer culture is to this borough of New York.

Which Brooklyn Breweries Are The Best?

Brooklyn, New York, has seen a rise in the number of new regional breweries opening up during the last ten years. Everyone can find something in Brooklyn, from household brands like Brooklyn Brewery to niche businesses like Other Half. And choosing which breweries to visit might be difficult with so many fantastic alternatives. We made this list of Brooklyn's Best Breweries for that reason.

Visit these Brooklyn, New York breweries for a fantastic craft beer experience. You won't be let down!

The Best Breweries in Brooklyn

Let's get started, shall we? The top Brooklyn craft breweries are listed here!

Brooklyn Brewery

The Brooklyn Brewery has been present since Brooklyn's craft brew sector first emerged, and now it is an internationally recognized, award-winning brewery. Both indoor and outdoor seats are available in their dog-friendly Williamsburg taproom. They provide tours of their plant so you can learn more about the inventive procedures used to make each beer.

Brooklyn Brewery offers a wide selection of fantastic non-alcoholic beers and seltzers on tap for those who don't drink craft beer. There are always exciting activities when you visit this famous Brooklyn brewery, including weekly quiz nights and bingo.

Phone: (718) 486-7422

Brooklyn, New York 11249, 79 N. 11th St.

Try the hazy IPA Pulp Art.

Other Half Brewing Company

There are five taprooms operated by Other Half Brewing in New York and one each in Philadelphia and Washington. But it all started at the Centre Street location! The magic began in 2014 at the junction of Carroll Gardens, Red Hook, and Gowanus, and they're still dishing out some of the most excellent craft beer in New York today from that original site.

Although they offer a wide range of beers, they are most recognized for their IPAs. You must stop by Other Half Brewing if you like hazy IPAs, or American IPAs, or want to try their Green Power Imperial IPA. They also provide a variety of flavor-filled seltzers under the brand name Oh2.

Phone: (212) 564-6065

195 Centre St., Brooklyn, New York 11231. the United States

Try these beers: Green Gates IPA and Rustic Pale Lager.

Six Point Brewing

Although Sixpoint Brewery is not a newcomer to craft beer, its taproom most surely is! Six point Brewery, established in the Red Hook neighborhood in 2004, has produced exceptional beers for the Brooklyn community, fine-tuning and enhancing with every batch. The community was beyond excited when their first official taproom opened on City Point BKLYN's lower level in October 2022.

Phone: (718) 861-0100

Location: 445 Gold Street, Brooklyn, New York 11201, the United States

Resin IPA and Scream Sickle IPA are two beers to try.

Threes Brewing

Residents and tourists adore the great Brooklyn Brewery Threes Brewing in the Gowanus neighborhood. Their taproom is connected to Ninth Street Espresso and offers delicious cuisine from a temporary food vendor named The Meat Hook. The brewery's primary specialties are lagers, hop-forward American ales, and mixed-culture beers. They use contemporary techniques to make traditional-style beers. Additionally, Threes Brewing offers a rewards program where you may accumulate points for each dollar spent and exchange them for beer money.

Phone: (718) 568-9673

Location: 333 Douglass Street, Brooklyn, New York 11217, USA

Beers to Try: Concentration

Brewery in Coney Island

The sole brewery on Coney Island is the Coney Island Brewery, which is a terrific stop on your trip out there. They give brewery tours and host weekly events like music trivia, live music, and special performances. Their outside beer garden section features activities like cornhole and picnic tables. Although they don't provide table service, you may order from their extensive meal menu and drink at the bar.

Phone: (718) 996-0019

Location: 1904 Surf Avenue, Brooklyn, NY 11224, USA

Try the Mermaid Pilsner beer.

Grimm Craft Beers

Joe and Lauren Grimm, a husband and wife team, established the excellent brewery, Grimm Artisanal Ales. Since outgrowing their home brewing system, they are the brains behind the brewing enterprise and have accomplished incredible things.

On the weekends, the taproom in East Williamsburg offers a variety of culinary pop-ups, and soon they'll be selling their wood-fired pizza! It is a lovely place to spend a day in Brooklyn since it has an industrial-chic ambiance inside, large windows that allow in loads of natural light, bookcases loaded with art books, and vinyl record players.

Phone: (718) 564-9767

Location: 990 Metropolitan Avenue, Brooklyn, New York 11211, USA

Cherry Raspberry Pop Beer is a Beer to Try!

Spirits of Interboro and Ales

East Williamsburg's Interboro Spirits and Ales is a brewery and distillery that offers draft beer, craft beer, cocktail cans, and house-made spirits to suit everyone's tastes. Both indoor and outdoor dining is available in their tasting area, which features a relaxed atmosphere and creative graffiti. You can also look closely at the magic behind the scenes by touring their brewing and distilling facilities.

Phone: (877) 843-6545

Located at 942 Grand Street, Brooklyn, New York 11211 the, United States

Try the Stay G-O-L-D IPA beer.

TALEA Beer Co.

TALEA beer is a women-owned brewery to increase the market for craft beers by developing brews that are simple to consume and have a fruity flavor profile. Cobble Hill and Williamsburg sites provide entertaining weekly activities, including Saturday yoga lessons.

Address: 87 Richardson St, Brooklyn, NY 11211

Phone: (347) 799-1281 the United States

Wheels up Beers to Try

Randolph Beer

There are two sites for Randolph Beer, each in Williamsburg and Dumbo. Their Dumbo site is unique since it has a gorgeous rooftop terrace available on the weekends, 12 stories above the brewery. Enjoy a craft beer or a unique beverage while taking in the stunning views of the city.

However, Randolph Beer is fantastic all year round. Their year-round basement taproom is a terrific spot to meet up with old friends and create new ones over a love of tasty beer. They offer many activities to keep you occupied, from traditional games like foosball and shuffleboard to obscure ones like Feather bowl.

Phone: (347) 280-3071

Location: 82 Prospect Street, Brooklyn, New York 11201, USA

Try Orange You Lovely beer.

Brooklyn Finback

After a successful launch in Queens, Finback created a second site in Brooklyn. Because of Finback's enthusiastic and skilled brew masters, every beer they make is excellent and worth drinking. You may discover a fantastic selection of foods, including some of the tastiest dumplings you've ever had, that are well coupled with their outstanding beer selections. You can guarantee a nice night out by adding a warm environment and stunning décor to the mix.

Phone: (347) 227-8008

545 President Street, Brooklyn, New York 11215 the, United States

The Dead Pecan and Rolling In Clouds IPA are two beers to try.

Brewery Five Boroughs Co.

At Five Boroughs Brewing, we prioritize authenticity, community, and excellence. Their Sunset Park brewery is a beautiful location for beer fans to unwind, unwind, and drink some fine craft brews. It is family- and pet-friendly. Each of their house-brewed beers is inspired by one of the five boroughs of New York City and the people who call it home. They provide a changing selection of seasonal and experimental brews, including sour beers, pastry stouts, lagers, and ales, in addition to their year-round favorites.

Phone: (718) 355-8575

In Brooklyn, New York, 11220, at 215 47th St., the United States

Try this beer: Tiny Juicy IPA

Kings County Brewers Collective

Kings County Brewers Collective has regularly ranked among the top brewers in Brooklyn for more than 40 years. They were the first brewery to start in the Bushwick district after Prohibition. They offer a dozen or more specialty beers on tap, cans, and bottles, all with funny names and highly imaginative artwork. A mainstay of the Brooklyn beer scene and one that should be noticed is King County Brewers.

Phone: (929) 409-5040

Location: 381 Troutman St, Brooklyn, New York 11237, USA

Beers to Try: Sidekicks of Superheroes

Evil Twin Brewing

A broad range of excellent beers is produced by Evil Twin Brewing, including several milkshake-style IPAs, hazy IPAs, sour ales, pale ales, and hard seltzers that you must try. The older of the two, located in Queens' Ridgewood district, is their DUMBO taproom. Both places offer a spacious, airy feel ideal for a chilled afternoon beverage.

Address: 43 Main St, Brooklyn, NY 11201, USA

Dr. Jepper Sour Beer

Brewery Strong Rope

All of the materials Strong Rope Brewery uses in its brews are entirely from New York, setting them apart from other Brooklyn brewers. The freshest vegetables, fruits, herbs, and spices make handmade local and organic ales and seasonal offerings, showcasing New York State farmers and maltsters.

Three of their taprooms in New York often hold events like trivia, live music, and food trucks that come and go. Strong Rope Brewery, a winning brewery that has received prizes in the Indie Beer Cup and the SMaSH Beer Competition, is an absolute must-visit.

Phone: (929) 337-8699

574a President Street, Brooklyn, New York 11215 the United States

Try these Beers: Leather

The Greenpoint Beer & Ale Co

Small batch brewing gives Greenpoint Beer & Ale Co.'s tasty beer plenty of possibilities for experimenting with new recipes and adjusting to tried-and-true ones. Brooklyn beer enthusiasts use rooftop terraces often, particularly on gorgeous sunny days. Choose a well-brewed German beer and one of their nibbles or burgers for a delicious combination.

Phone: (347) 725-3061

Location: 1150 Manhattan Avenue, Brooklyn, New York 11222, USA

Try this beer: Greenpoint Witte

Brunch Spots

Best Brunch Spots in Brooklyn

At the top brunch places in Brooklyn, enjoy sweet and savory dishes that combine breakfast and lunch while sipping coffee and mimosas.

Brunch is not only the best meal in the world but also shares first place with breakfast, lunch, dinner, and snack time. It's also the most popular social gathering of the weekend, far better than date night. New York City excels at brunch more than any other city. Brunch is about gossip, sauces made with egg yolks, and drinking before noon. With many alternatives to fill your sweet 48 weekend hours with fantastic foods and beverages, Brooklyn has a firm grasp on the genre.

Leland Eating and Drinking House

Trout raclette and charred lemon skillet mussels are just a few of the supper menu dishes Leland offers during brunch, along with a few more specialties only available on the weekend. SECs on Hawaiian rolls with pickled jalapenos, fried squid sandwiches, and babka French toast are just a few of the brunch-specific appetizers available. The most significant time to buy delicious baked products like Leland's homemade sourdough cinnamon buns is now.

New York, NY 11238 755 Dean Street

Open from 10 am to 4 pm on Sunday, from 5 pm to 10 pm on Wednesday and Thursday, from 1 pm to 4 pm, and from 5 pm on Friday.

Second Henry Public

Popular Henry Public receives a gentle saloon patina from Brooklyn thanks to light Olde Weste components. Customers can see it's attractive outside dining shed from half a block away. The bar and rear dining area also have a more general wood feel. In addition to additional eggs anyway and the finest turkey leg sandwich you've ever had, the filling bacon, egg, and cheese are offered in various formats.

Brooklyn, NY 11201 329 Henry St

Between Pacific St. and Atlantic Ave., there is a crossroads.

Contact Information: 718-852-8630

Mon–Thu, 5pm–2am; Fri, 5pm–4am; Sat, noon–4am; Sun, noon–2am

Rana Fifteen

Terrific Family-style prix fixe feasts with the restaurant's signature fifteen dishes are served at Rana Fifteen in Park Slope, near Gowanus. A variety of jams, fresh fruit, and preserves are included in the breakfast spread, along with eggs prepared in one of two ways, spicy beef sujuk, potatoes with leeks, cheese, and olives, and light asthma.

NYC 11217 209 4th Avenue

Contact Information: 347-599-1525

Saturday and Sunday from 11 am to 3 pm, Friday and Saturday from 5 pm to 11 pm, Sunday, Wednesday, and Thursday from 5 pm to 10 pm.

Inga's Bar

This quaint eatery is situated on a picturesque brownstone Brooklyn street and is as dramatic as they come. Lovely latkes with smoked salmon, sour cream, and trout roe, gluten-free pancakes, egg and non-egg sandwiches, omelets, and the delicious celery Victor that was initially featured on Inga's supper menu when it first debuted last year are all available for brunch.

NYC 11201, 66 Hicks Street

Wednesday through Sunday, starting at 5 pm

Kokomo Restaurants,

Williamsburg

Choose from chicken and waffles, sweet plantain pancakes, and saltfish avocado toast in Kokomo's resort-chic setting. To get over any oncoming scares, you can enjoy Sunday brunch all day long with unique cocktails.

Contact information

 65 Kent Avenue

Brooklyn

347-799-1312.

Operating hours: Tuesday through Thursday, 4 pm to 11 pm; Friday through Sunday, 11 am to 11 pm

Alma

Climb the two floors to Alma's rooftop for lunch with a view. It's so gorgeous that if you're sitting near the windows, folks may occasionally come too close while attempting to take a picture. Having an affair would also be a horrible spot since you would almost certainly end up in the backdrop of 100 candid photos. But a new type of spark might be started by its fantastic fish tacos, enchiladas, fiery sauces, and margaritas.

187 Columbia St

Brooklyn, New York

11231-4

Contact: 718-643-5400

Open from Mon-Thu 5:30 pm-10 pm, Fri 5–11 pm, Sat 11 am-11 pm, and Sun 11 am-10 pm.

French Louie

This posh, sparkling location on Atlantic Avenue is fresh and welcoming both inside and out on the terrace. The brunch menu includes dishes like a tutu-shaped egg dish, crème brûlée French toast, scrambles, salads, and the customary spiked morning drinks.

Brooklyn 11207, 320 Atlantic Avenue

Contact: 718-935-1200

Open daily from 5 to 11 pm.

Chapter Six: Shopping in Brooklyn

Independent Boutiques

It's no wonder shopping followed suit, as Brooklyn has recently emerged as a destination for some of New York City's most lavish hotels, restaurants, and bars. There is intense competition since there are stores on almost every corner, but we considered all the possibilities to choose the finest of the best. Check out these seven eccentric, stylish, and distinctive stores for the ultimate Brooklyn boutique shopping binge.

Concrete + Water

Concrete + Water, a plant-filled Williamsburg store specializing in comfortable, breezy indoor-meets-outdoor decor, blends Brooklyn with the West Coast. Founded by D.J. and nightlife veteran JD Gluckstern and stylist Hannah Dilworth, the store sells some of the area's top menswear, women swear, and home products. Favorite brands and products include cheeky bath mats from Cold Picnic, casual sweatshirts from Paloma Wool, small-batch perfume from Fiele Fragrances, and vegan leather puffers from Nanushka.

Sincerely, Tommy

Sincerely, Tommy is a women wear and lifestyle concept shop in Bed-Stuy that offers high-end clothing and a side of regional fair trade coffee. Warm up with a honey latte from the shop's S, T Coffee bar, which uses Brooklyn roaster Cafe Grumpy beans, before you hit the racks. Then spend the rest of the day browsing new companies like Victoria Mingot, which makes 24k gold earrings in Denmark, Alfeya Valeria, which sells mules made of mohair fur, and Menos Mas Skincare, which sells Matcha Mint masks.

Consignment Brooklyn

At Boerum Hill's Consignment Brooklyn, established by Eva Dayton, you can buy and sell modern designer apparel, footwear, and accessories in brand-new or outstanding condition. Since there is just one of each item and the business doesn't accept holds, check out the shop's

Instagram page to get a sense of its aesthetic before heading there as soon as possible.

Collyer's Mansion

In Brooklyn Heights, Collyer's Mansion, home items take center stage. You may buy colorful Italian-designed quilts by Lisa Corti, unique artwork and prints by many artists, antique carpets, eco-friendly furniture by Fermob, and much more at this eclectic, quirky boutique. Nearly everything in the store lives up to the store's tagline, "world of color, print, and pattern"; there isn't a boring item in sight.

Bird

Talking about Brooklyn boutiques would only be complete by mentioning Bird, which in 1999 practically popularized the phrase. The eco-conscious fashion destination has four locations in the borough now—Cobble Hill, Fort Greene, Park Slope, and the Williamsburg flagship—and offers area-specific collections that reflect each district's distinct look. If you can only visit one, go to the Williamsburg location. It is the first retail space in New York to get the coveted LEED-CI Gold certification, and it has to change art exhibits in its LEED-certified Gold store.

Swords-Smith

Swords-Smith, an airy boutique that debuted in 2013 and is located in Williamsburg, prides itself on its careful selection. The shop bursts with distinctive menswear, women's wear, and accessories, emphasizing contemporary, imaginative designers. The store is the most excellent place in town to build your unique personal style, offering everything from sculptural footwear by shoemaker Gray Matters to oversized denim turtlenecks by Marfa-based designer Ashley Rowe.

O.N.A

O.N.A., which opened in Prospect Heights in 2012, has established itself as a destination store for sustainable and ethically produced apparel and accessories. Come in to purchase Brooklyn-based Dusen Dusen's imaginatively printed t-shirts and dresses, Ilana Kohn's relaxed jumpsuits and coveralls, and Kordal's premium knitwear.

Vintage Shops

Best Brooklyn Vintage Shops

Broadway Fashion

1227 Broadway

Broadway Fashion, in the heart of Bushwick, is our top recommendation for secondhand shops in Brooklyn. You may get some of the fundamental necessities for your outfit at this Brooklyn secondhand store at a reasonable price

Both women's and men's clothing are available here. For ladies, there is a vast assortment of blouses and dresses, while for guys, there are many different T-shirts, hoodies, and slacks. For each, there is a variety of shoes and sneakers.

Although you won't find anything high-end here, this location is as inexpensive as they get. There are items as little as $6. Take your time; there is a lot to choose from.

While you're here, visit the other top-notch Bushwick thrift shops to find the finest bargains in Brooklyn.

New Brooklyn Fashion

1065 Broadway

This hidden treasure and fantastic location for thrifting in Brooklyn are also in Bushwick, only a few streets from Broadway Fashion. If you're searching for a very excellent price, this is a beautiful place to start regarding Brooklyn Vintage stores.

This Brooklyn vintage boutique has a wide selection of colorful and vibrantly colored apparel for the seasons, focusing on women's clothing (dresses, blouses, and shirts).

Ideal for spring and summer. In the rear, there is a smaller area with men's apparel. Mostly T-shirts and jeans.

This location is quite reasonably priced. Certain items cost just $5. Give this store a look-see if you want a lovely summer sundress.

Also, check out all the other top things to do in Bushwick while in the area.

Brooklyn Brick House Vintage

521 Grand Street

Both men's and women's clothing may be found in plenty at this Brooklyn vintage store in Williamsburg. The men's area has an extensive selection of vintage t-shirts, button-down shirts, and excellent denim.

For the ladies, there is a choice of vintage shirts, dresses, and jeans.

You could spend some time browsing through their vintage shirts at this store since the pricing is cheap, given that you're in Williamsburg.

Once the weather drops, this is also an excellent place to get a stylish vintage or used jacket.

Le Point Value

321 Clarkson Avenue

Le Point Value, which has sites across the five boroughs, is another contender for the title of a most reasonably priced thrift shop in Brooklyn with its Prospect Lefferts Gardens location.

This Brooklyn vintage store offers a warehouse of men's, women's, and kids' apparel. You may find almost every kind of essential item of clothing here, making it a veritable apparel paradise.

Le Point has many apparel and accessory options, so you could spend hours browsing through them.

You won't find the hottest labels or well-known names here like in the last two shops. However, it will be difficult not to discover anything worthwhile to grab if you take the time to sift through the enormous sea of things.

Green Village Used Furniture & Clothing

276 Starr Street

Speaking about massive antique shops in Brooklyn, Green Village is another area in Bushwick where you could spend hours browsing. It's a prominent place. Huge warehouse.

It's all in the name when it comes to what they have to offer; in addition to vintage apparel for both men and women, this shop also sells a wide variety of household products, including furniture and antiques, so you can be sure to discover excellent deals for your house as well as for yourself.

Searching through this shop will undoubtedly be difficult, but Green Village is worth the patience and the work; allow yourself additional time to peruse their inventory!

Monk Vintage

496 Driggs Avenue.

This Williamsburg secondhand shop is a well-liked Brooklyn vintage hangout on Driggs Avenue. You may discover a fantastic, well-chosen variety of Brooklyn vintage apparel at Monk Vintage, which in my view, more than any other, appears to have the ideal balance of old and fashionable clothing.

The business also offers artwork, antiques, and old movie posters at the checkout area as a bonus.

Additionally, you may donate your gently used clothing items in exchange for a 25% discount on your subsequent purchase.

Additionally, this Brooklyn vintage shop does a very decent job of offering a wide variety of men's and women's apparel for each of the four seasons. Therefore, Monk Vintage provides everything you need, whether you're searching for a winter coat or shoes for the beach.

Brooklyn Woke Vintage

158 Bedford Ave

I'll point you toward Brooklyn Woke Vintage, another Williamsburg treasure and a fantastic place to browse for vintage items in Brooklyn. For those who grew up in the 1980s and 1990s, Brooklyn Woke will undoubtedly be a particular pleasure.

Many vintage and antique items may be found at this store. They have retro vinyl albums, cassette tapes, action figures (WWE, Star Wars), antique cameras, and even radios and CD players in the 80s manner. If you're old enough, you can even find PEZheads there.

The pricing is relatively fair given these objects' scarcity and excellent condition.

You may also bring in your unique vintage goods, which they may purchase based on the item and its condition.

The apparel options for men and women are limited, but the primary attractions here unquestionably are the old toys and antiques. If you get the opportunity, be sure to visit this location!

Brooklyn Flea

Our second choice for Brooklyn's most fabulous vintage shops is more of an outdoor flea market than a physical business. The Brooklyn Flea is that market.

There are four venues for this flea market, including those in Brooklyn and Manhattan's Lower East Side and Chelsea.

The DUMBO site is at 80 Pearl Street, beneath the Manhattan Bridge archway, and is open on Sundays from 10 am until 5 pm.

Sundays from 10 am to 5 pm, the Williamsburg location is at Kent Avenue and North 6th Street (51 N. 6th Street).

Of the venues thus far listed, this market provides the broadest selection of goods. Vendors offer a variety of interests in addition to vintage apparel for men and women, including face masks, furniture, antiques, and Pokémon cards.

Additionally, this market permits regional artists to sell their works, allowing you to check out what some of the city's up-and-coming artist's offer.

The costs are reasonable; nothing is outrageous. The search is very swift and straightforward in Williamsburg. An excellent place to visit on a pleasant spring or summer day!

Bookstores

The Brooklyn's Best Bookstores

Each shop is unquestionably worthwhile if you ever find yourself in New York. Spend a day in Williamsburg and enjoy some literary treats.

Quimby's Bookstore

This Brooklyn bookstore on Metropolitan Avenue specializes in a small collection of liberal fiction and non-fiction. Most of the current events books in this department are categorized by race, LGBTQ, New York focus, and even a punk section.

The shop is stocked with wonderful small things that may be purchased, like mugs, enamel pins, tote bags, and more. These goods brazenly display phrases like "Kittens Against Trump," "Black Lives Matter," and other current-event or literary puns. Additionally, the business has some red wall art.

Ben's Book

Ben's Books, a charming and adorable tiny establishment with only one room devoted to the prettier side of literature, is located around the corner from Quimby's.

A poetry department, books on sex and sexuality, books on essays, large volumes on art and art history, and some gorgeous versions of sci-fi classics may all be found in this store.

This book store caters to students, stocking anything the booksellers find interesting.

While you browse, classical music plays in the background. Tarot cards, Tamagotchis, and even a small record collection are available.

Spoonbill and Sugartown

Yes, this is the perfect name for a bookshop.

This type of jack-of-all-trades bookshop, which sells new and old books, is adjacent to a retail center called The Mini Mall in Brooklyn (which also has thrift shops, Coco bubble tea, and a tattoo parlor).

Spoonbill likely has what you're searching for since it is less specialized and more typical.

We overheard a father and his elementary-aged kid discussing and contrasting the writing styles of George Orwell and Maya Angelou, which was the most endearing part of our visit to the shop. What a sweet moment, I wish I had captured it in a bottle.

McNally Jackson

In reality, McNally Jackson is one of four independent bookshops scattered around Brooklyn and Manhattan. It is the group's most significant and conventional, but that doesn't mean it lacks charm.

The most recent hardcover fiction is prominently displayed as you approach this bookshop, which has everything you'd expect. But this store's categorization decision—they arrange their books by region—is excellent and deserving of celebration!

It's all arranged by region, whether you're seeking Latin American, Middle Eastern, or East Asian literature. It could not be a welcome sight as readers increasingly seek out literature from outside their own countries and languages (hence the presence of this site).

Simply outstanding. They also print staff picks on little tags, like our favorite English bookshops in Bath, Mr. B's Emporium, and Topping & Co.

Book Thug Nation

When I announced the most excellent bookshop name, maybe I spoke too soon.

The calm, cozy area known as Book Thug Nation is crammed with only previously owned literary literature.

It was explained to me by the attractive young woman behind the counter that this shop prioritized the purchasing and sale of literary fiction, award-winning novels, classic literature, and other works of actual quality.

Independent comic books like Top Shelf and Image are available in the shop. While there, I picked up a secondhand edition of John Kennedy Toole's A Confederacy of Dunces. Cheers to reading!

Record Stores

For audiophiles throughout the city, Brooklyn has become a hidden treasure. The most significant record shops in Brooklyn feature enormous selections of new and old LPs, making it easy to locate your preferred genre.

Brooklyn offers a variety of experiences; some record shops are modest but have some scarce vinyl, while others are enormous and have collections like libraries. One of the biggest shops in the city itself is located in the borough!

On your next visit to a record shop, think about taking the train and seeing what the most populous borough of New York City offers regarding musical experiences. Still, trying to figure out where to begin? Are you a newcomer to the area? Check out our list of the top record shops in Brooklyn to get all the information you need to start your collection.

HIFI Provisions

HiFi Provisions is a music business that just recently opened in 2021 and specializes in antique audio, including vinyl records and record players. For instance, audio equipment from McIntosh, Fisher, ProAc, and Pro-Ject is readily available throughout the shop. They may also buy speakers, vinyl, and turntables at HiFi Provisions.

This shop is a testament to Matthew Coluccio's affection for it. There are wooden racks outside with a variety of record treasures on them. There are more recent LPs among the antique ones, too. Don't be shocked if you see one of Matthew's audio tinkering projects—which often include analog tube amps—in the warm atmosphere of the whole shop. You shouldn't be shocked if you find something genuinely unique since Coluccio is renowned for his propensity to travel for rare albums. Except for classical albums, there is music for almost any musical pr

Public Record

Public Records is where you may locate your favorite LPs while listening to live or vinyl-recorded music. It's a local tribute to the growth of music bars in Tokyo. Henry Rich, a local restaurateur, caters to Public Records, which offers cocktails, vegan meals, and non-alcoholic beverages. Explore the Sound Room's vast collection of records and look at the vinyl record players for sale, including Pro-Ject models.

The Sound Room is renowned for its frequent, small-scale concerts. Public Records is a genre-neutral store where you may find pressings from several artists on numerous record labels. Live performance styles will also change from day to day. The architecture of the space also supports aural integrity; whether music is played live or on a vinyl record player, it vibrates with a clarity ideal for audiophiles seeking their next immersive experience.

Black Gold Records

On Carroll Gardens' Court Street is a little, cozy record store called Black Gold Records. Although they don't have a vast record library, they have some exciting vinyl, including Motown oldies. As you browse the store, you will see that they also offer vintage and antique products.

Because it doubles as a coffee shop, this establishment differentiates itself from the other record shops in Brooklyn. At Black Gold Records, it's simple to lose track of time while enjoying some music and excellent brew.

Academy Record Annex

The Academy Record Annex, a record store with the most incredible assortment in New York City, is situated on Oak Street in Greenpoint. In addition to having an extensive selection of vinyl, this store is a great location to buy unique souvenirs for certain bands, such as t-shirts and posters. Even periodicals exist there that include stories about musicians.

In this Brooklyn music store, you may also discover artwork created by local artists and artwork from other countries. Whatever you are looking for, the vinyl is well-organized, so if they have a copy of the record you want for sale, locating it should be simple.

Earwax Records

One of Brooklyn's most well-known record businesses, Earwax Records, is among the oldest in Williamsburg. The shop opened in 1990 and has new and old records across all genres. To round out your library, they provide a variety of timeless songs from the 1960s and 1970s, as well as more modern music. This shop also sells old-style record players if you need one.

The proprietor has been a professional DJ for over 40 years. Therefore he has a passion for music that only die-hard fans would comprehend. Look for handwritten notes detailing some of the recordings for sale if you are in the store.

Brooklyn's Record Exchange

Bush wick's Brooklyn Record Exchange was once known as Co-Op 87. If you like funk and soul albums, this is one of the most significant record shops to visit. They provide a wide variety, many of which are just a few dollars. Bring your headphones so you can listen to the music, please!

You may find vinyl records for your collection at Material World Records if you seek hardcore, avant-garde, or punk music. They even offer a variety of tapes you may listen to.

You may buy, sell, and exchange vinyl records at Vinyl Fantasy. They offer historical and independent DC and Marvel comics and jazz, punk, classic, and indie bands at their venue.

Since the 1990s, Park Slope has been home to Music Matters, a record shop. They feature an extensive collection of cassette tapes, CDs, and vinyl records. Even some hardware is on hand in case you need it while there.

Human Head Records in East Williamsburg offers every kind of record, including reggae, jazz, 80s dance, and prog rock. Additionally, they provide turntable repairs and brushes for cleaning records before playing them.

Second-Hand Records NYC is an excellent location to start if you want to hear live music in Bushwick since it has a studio in the rear of the shop. They provide a wide variety of hip-hop, jazz, rock, and funk LPs for sale, both new and old.

Flea Markets

If you want to locate antique items reasonably priced, go to Brooklyn's flea markets. You can find almost anything in Brooklyn, including enormous Levi's denim jackets, rare vintage LPs, and an engraved silver harp from the early 1940s. Given the vast options Brooklyn alone offers, you may have to sift through some trash. But rest assured—it will be worthwhile!

Six Of Brooklyn's Top Flea Markets Have Been Narrowed Down From The Original List:

Brooklyn Flea Dumbo - Brooklyn's Dumbo

In less than ten years, the Brooklyn Flea market has grown to be the most well-known in Brooklyn and maybe all of New York City. In DUMBO today, Brooklyn Flea runs an outdoor market with around 80 sellers. Brooklyn Flea is a terrific place to find genuine antique items and is conveniently located in DUMBO, just under the Manhattan Bridge. It also serves as a perfect reason to explore a typical Brooklyn neighborhood. Vintage clothes, jewelry, collectibles, furniture, and antiques are just a few items vendors sell. Brooklyn Flea would only fall short with artisanal goods made by regional artists and delectable cuisine-stay strong.

Brooklyn Flea

Sundays from April through October

Time: 10 am to 5 pm.

Location: 80 Pearl Street, Brooklyn, New York, beside the Manhattan Bridge Archway

Brooklyn Flea Holiday & Winter Market in Fort Greene, Brooklyn (New York City)

Brooklyn Flea becomes the Brooklyn Flea Winter Market from November through March when it relocates inside. The flea market and Smorgasburg, the most popular culinary event in the US, are combined within the Atlantic Center in Fort Greene. It makes the Christmas market a fantastic location to locate distinctive presents and indulge in delectable cuisine simultaneously. Remember that this site now has more food vendors than vintage and antique retailers. The flea market area currently has roughly 20 merchants offering high-quality mid-century modern furniture, vintage clothing, handcrafted items, and more.

Winter & Holiday Market at Brooklyn Flea

When: November through March, on Saturdays and Sundays.

Hours: 11 am to 6 pm (5 pm on Sunday)

Location: The Atlantic Center is 625 Atlantic Avenue in Brooklyn, New York

Williamsburg, Brooklyn (NYC) Brooklyn Flea Record Fair

Vintage record enthusiasts' hearts are racing because of this occasion. Brooklyn Flea hosts the Brooklyn Flea Record Fair around three times each year. Aside from Smorgasburg at East River State Park, more than 50 sellers of old vinyl records, CDs, and cassettes set up shop on this occasion. The Brooklyn Flea record fair has a considerably smaller winter version. With roughly 14 specialty exhibitors, it coexists with the Brooklyn Flea Winter Market.

Record Fair at Brooklyn Flea

When: Three times each year on Saturdays and Sundays. Hours are 11 am to 8 pm (5 pm on Sunday).

Location: Atlantic Center in the winter or East River State Park in the summer, Brooklyn, New York

Artists & Fleas Williamsburg: Brooklyn's Williamsburg (New York City)

One of the first of its type in Brooklyn, I'm Williamsburg, Flea Market. I was established by Artists & Fleas. Shoppers may find items made by upcoming neighborhood artists and craftspeople at this indoor market in Williamsburg in a welcoming and enjoyable setting. The Williamsburg Flea Market offers shopping for vintage home decor, vinyl records, books, antiques, clothing, accessories, and artwork and design. The Brooklyn weekend flea market known as Artists & Fleas has become so well-liked over time that there are now two daily flea markets in Manhattan (Artists & Fleas Chelsea Market and another one in SoHo) and one in Los Angeles.

Williamsburg's Artists & Fleas

When: Saturday and Sunday, 10:00–19:00, 10 am till 7 pm.

Location: 70 North Street, Brooklyn's Williamsburg

The Oddities Flea Market in Greenpoint, Brooklyn, New York

Visit this bizarre flea market in Greenpoint immediately if you're searching for something odd and unique. The main attractions of Oddities Flea Market are anatomical oddities, artifacts from natural and medical history, taxidermy, and one-of-a-kind objects. At Brooklyn's Oddities Flea Market, you can get everything from taxidermy to handcrafted jewelry to skulls and fortune-telling tea cups. Oddities Flea Market has sellers from all across the country, which results in a brilliant and fascinating range of goods. At the Brooklyn Bazaar, the flea market is held on three levels at least once yearly.

Strange Flea Market

When: sporadically

Location: 150 Greenpoint Ave, Brooklyn, NYC, home of the Brooklyn Bazaar

Metro Flea NYC - Brooklyn's Park Slope

The ideal place to explore one of Brooklyn's hippest districts is Metro Flea NYC in Park Slope, Brooklyn. This market has been a staple of Park Slope for more than three decades. Visitors will discover various handcrafted carpets, baskets, and jewelry, among antique items. Vintage vinyl records, antique cameras, bicycles, kitchenware, furniture, and other vintage finds are available at this New York City market. A recent addition to Park Slope's weekend schedule is the Metro Flea NYC 5th Avenue, just a short walk from the Metro Flea NYC 7th Avenue.

7th Avenue Metro Flea in NYC

Saturday and Sunday, 9 am to 6 pm

180 7th Avenue, between 1st and 2nd Street, is the location. 350 Fifth Avenue, Brooklyn, NY 11215, and Brooklyn, NY 11215

139 | BROOKLYN TRAVEL GUIDE 2023

Chapter Seven: Events and Festivals in Brooklyn

Brooklyn Book Festival

At the Brooklyn Book Festival in September, authors and readers from all over the globe assemble. The Festival comprises 7-day Bookend Events, a Children's Day, and a Festival Day with more than 300 writers and 250 booksellers mingling at the outdoor Literary Marketplace. It features several literary luminaries from across the world as well as up-and-coming authors. Thousands of book enthusiasts are undoubtedly drawn to this unusual and varied gathering. Joan Didion, Salman Rushdie, Dennis Lehane, John Reed, Rosanne Cash, Karl Ove Knausgrd, Dave Eggers, Rumaan Alam, Martin Amis, Laura Lippmann, Tayari Jones, Akwaeke Emezi, Greg Pardlo, A.M. Homes, April Ryan, Alexander Chee, and many more have all been at the Festival in previous years.

Brooklyn Borough President Marty Markowitz and co-producers Liz Koch and Carolyn Greer established the

Brooklyn Book Festival in 2006. Since many authors call Brooklyn their home, the event aims to highlight the "Brooklyn voice" in writing. A literary prize of US$50,000 was created by St. Francis College in 2009 to encourage a writer in the middle of their career; the Brooklyn Book Festival author jury selects the recipient.

Over 30,000 people attend the Festival, drawn by its literary-themed activities, panel discussions, book signings, vendors, stand-up acts, and performances in different public spaces.

Brooklyn Film Festival

An annual worldwide celebration of independent cinema from all over the globe, the Brooklyn Cinema Festival. The Festival, which has been going on since 1997, is regarded as one of the most significant venues for independent cinema in New York. Over 120 feature, documentary, animation, and experimental films are shown at the Festival each.

All screenings are part of the Brooklyn Film Festival's holistic celebration of filmmaking craft, including panel discussions, hands-on workshops, and special events, including Filmmakers' Dinners, live music, and panel discussions.

The Brooklyn Film Festival takes pride in its wide range of films from established and up-and-coming directors, many of which are seldom seen in mainstream cinemas. The Festival is a crucial setting for filmmakers to discover their audience and earn exposure.

The annual Brooklyn Film Award honors and rewards filmmakers for their efforts and is presented as part of the Brooklyn Film Festival. The awards presentation, which takes place on the Festival's last night, is a special occasion for everyone involved.

The Brooklyn Film Festival gives indie films an unmatched platform for promotion.

Festival of Afro-Punk

Brooklyn, New York, hosts the multi-day Afropunk Festival every year. The Festival, a celebration of blackness, creativity, and culture, draws visitors from all over the globe for a weekend of performances, exhibitions, and seminars. It serves as a forum for established and up-

and-coming artists, intellectuals, and activists engaged in the constantly developing worldwide movement of resistance to repressive regimes.

The Afropunk Festival's creators sought to provide a secure environment for the black community worldwide to express themselves and start a dialogue on important topics. Despite having a solid punk rock foundation, the event welcomes music from all genres, including established artists and up-and-coming musicians.

The event features more than simply music. Panel discussions and seminars are held where vital issues concerning the black community are covered. Authors, activists, and representatives of the entertainment sector are among the speakers who spark conversation and invite audience involvement.

All during the FestivalFestival, visual arts are on display for people who want to express themselves creatively. Artists are encouraged to display pieces, provide workshops that spark discourse, and foster an environment of admiration.

The Afropunk Festival provides a venue for stress relief and belonging to a more significant cause. The event aims to provide a welcoming and inviting environment where individuals may express themselves via music, art, and discussion.

Smorgasburg

Smorgasburg is a Brooklyn, New York, outdoor market for food and culture. Visitors may sample a wide range of foods from across the globe at Smorgasburg while also taking in art, music, and other cultural lifestyle experiences. The market was established in 2011 as an outdoor food market experiment and has since developed into one of Brooklyn's most famous culinary and cultural attractions.

A broad range of delectable foods is available in Smorgasburg from several vendors. There is food to suit every taste, from delicious Mexican street tacos to OK hot dogs. For a sweet treat, guests may choose from various handcrafted ice cream varieties at Smorgasburg's ice cream kiosk or sample one of the specialty coffee beverages.

Smorgasburg has a reasonably laid-back vibe since many attendees choose to lay on the grass and take in the sunshine. Music is often played Throughout the day, fostering a lively, joyful atmosphere. Additionally, visitors may participate in various cultural activities, including yoga and painting classes.

In terms of fashion, Smorgasburg has a lot to offer as well. Finding something special is simple since many sellers sell handcrafted, distinctive apparel and accessories. In addition, there are regularly unique occasions and pop-up stores that showcase fresh and intriguing goods.

Undoubtedly, one of Brooklyn's most popular attractions is Smorgasburg. Smorgasburg offers a variety of enjoyable experiences, whether you're seeking mouthwatering cuisine or intriguing merchants.

Since the late 18th century, New Year's Eve celebrations have included fireworks. The custom is said to have started in China when settlers celebrated the New Year by lighting firecrackers and bright paper lanterns. The usage of fireworks for celebrations quickly expanded to other regions, particularly in Europe and the US. These days, one of the most eagerly awaited aspects of New Year's Eve festivities throughout the globe is the use of pyrotechnics.

Fireworks on New Year's Eve are a beautiful way to welcome the New Year and provide luck and opportunities for everyone. Every year, musically accompanied multicolored sparks light up the sky in cities all around the globe, creating a spectacular show that never fails to inspire astonishment and excitement in everyone who witnesses it. Fireworks occur in various forms, dimensions, and hues, exploding over the night sky in different patterns.

The size and style of New Year's Eve fireworks may vary greatly depending on where you are in the globe. Each show is unique and unforgettable, from the magnificent Macy's fireworks in New York City to the low-impact "sunshine" fireworks in Australia so inhabitants do not disturb the local fauna. Although most New Year's Eve fireworks displays mark the beginning of a new year, many nations observe the occasion uniquely. For instance, in Japan, fireworks are used to keep the accession of the new Emperor.

Whatever your method of celebration, New Year's Eve fireworks are a classic and stunning way to bring in the new year. Take pleasure in every glimmer, every sound, and the excitement and optimism that come with a new year.

Chapter 8: Practical Information for Visitors

Getting Around Brooklyn

Recommended Transportation Options

Brooklyn shares New York City's reputation for having vast subterranean and public transit networks. Except for Red Hook and some areas of East Brooklyn, where you might want to consider bus transportation (these tend to be neighborhoods with pockets of crime, so if you can outright avoid these areas, it's best to do so anyway), the subway is the best way to get around Brooklyn.

The "Brooklyn Pub Crawl" is a self-guided tour of all the top pubs in the Park Slope area and is an excellent option if you're searching for some inventive methods to move about. Try the "Brooklyn Bridge Walk," a self-guided scenic trek between Manhattan and Brooklyn, for something more family-friendly.

Airports and Car Rentals

The JFK Airport and the LaGuardia Airport are excellent options for flights into New York City. LaGuardia and JFK are closer to Brooklyn's northwest and east, respectively, which is best depending on your destination inside Brooklyn and which provides cheaper flights from your departure airport.

While both airports provide several vehicle rental companies, we advise bypassing the rental at JFK in favor of boarding the AirTrain, an easy method to access the MTA New York City Transit subways, buses, and the Long Island Rail Road. You may ride the AirTrain from JFK to Jamaica Station in northern Brooklyn and the J or Z Subway. It takes around 50 minutes and costs $7.50.

Numerous public transportation options are also provided by LaGuardia, such as the $13 NYC Airporter, which makes stops at the Port Authority Bus Terminal, Grand Central Station, and Penn Station.

Accommodations in Brooklyn

Brooklyn has slowly developed into a location to be seen and seen in the last several years. Most visitors come to experience the borough's well-known hipster culture, which includes live music venues, art galleries, whiskey bars, and up-and-coming chefs. However, the actual benefit of staying in "B.K.," as the locals call it, is that you get more for your money.

Numerous hotels in New York City offer bigger rooms, roofs with breathtaking views of the Manhattan skyline, and introductions to some of the most fascinating creative talent in the city. No matter what you're looking for—a waterfront Williamsburg tower, a long-term inn in Greenpoint, or a grand brownstone in "Bed-Stuy"—we've got you covered.

Ace Hotel Brooklyn

Optimum for Music

The location of this Brooklyn property—which, upon opening, was the biggest for the brand—would always be significant for a business that enjoys establishing hotels in the newest "it" neighborhoods. By hosting the local musicians and artists who should be on the radar of every creative visitor, this boutique hotel is establishing itself as a barometer for what's hot in the borough. Instead of choosing commercialized Williamsburg, where other vibrant hospitality brands have set up shop, the hotel chose the residential outskirts of downtown, between leafy Boerum Hill and Fort Greene, close to the Barclays Center.

The Franklin Guesthouse

For Extended Stays

One of Brooklyn's best-kept secrets is this 30-key inn, just a few steps from Paulie Gee's, the renowned pizza joint in Greenpoint. This facility is all about creating a cozy atmosphere. It comprises roomy studios and suites that, between the art and the fully equipped kitchens, seem much more like lofts than hotel rooms. Along with going above and above, the staff is renowned for organizing goodbye cards and bringing over prescription medicines. It should come as no surprise that Franklin's is a top pick for seasoned New Yorkers, whether staying a while or simply having a fun trip.

1hotel Brooklyn Bridge

The Most Sustainable

The flagship of 1Hotels, a business that has emerged as the model for sustainability among luxury hotels, is this riverfront resort in Dumbo, which offers the most incredible views of the borough's most well-known landmark. Everything here has a back-story, whether it's Jarrod Beck's lobby sculpture made of rubber strips that were upstate New York tornadoes that blew off a rooftop or living walls made of endemic plants. In addition, the hotel adheres to LEED standards, uses greywater irrigation and wind power, and was constructed using 22% recycled and 32% local resources.

Akwaaba Mansion

History's Finest

This luxurious B&B in Bedford-Stuyvesant is co-owned by Monique Greenwood, the former editor-in-chief of Essence, which explains why it seems as if it were taken straight out of a glossy magazine. With 14-foot ceilings, beautiful fireplaces, and a thoughtful selection of antiques, fabrics, and artifacts from all across Africa, Greenwood painstakingly restored the 1860s "Bed-Stuy" house to create one of the neighborhood's most serene homes. Here, it's all about tradition and Afrocentric elegance: the four roomy suites are named after significant historical and cultural locations, and the inn's name, Akwaaba, is a Twi word for "welcome."

Henry Norman Hotel

The Best Hotel for Bon Viveur Is Henry Norman

Even the tiniest rooms have access corridors and high ceilings at this eccentric boutique hotel's industrial décor, which includes exposed pipes, masonry, and pressed-tin roofs. It is situated in Greenpoint and is a favorite with tourists and digital nomads who have already seen many of the city's attractions. Instead, the area is home to some of New York's cult pubs and eateries, which various celebrities prefer when they are not on the clock. Those planning to stay for a while should reserve the hotel's Loft Suite, which offers a kitchen.

Williamsburg Hotel,

Optimal For a Restful Night's Sleep

Let's face it, this city isn't renowned for being a pleasant place to sleep, especially when you're right in the center of energetic Williamsburg. So be sure to enjoy the rare moment of peace that such accommodations, Music machines, blackout curtains that block off the whole view of Manhattan, and cloud-like mattresses, with their unique features, provide a luxurious experience.

Provide. Just know that after you go, the celebration will resume; this city slicker is the life of the party.

Hotel Box House

Most Value

Forget the borough; this old factory is now among the hippest, most cheap lodgings in the whole city. This location offers excellent value for the money in the northernmost part of Greenpoint, which is close to the B.Q.E. where Brooklyn and Queens meet. Consider the hotel's oversized rooms, appealing design, waterfront views, and one of the finest midrange restaurant options in the area. Even the most cynical New Yorker will be impressed by its breakfast alone. Additionally, Dave, the house bartender, makes an Old Fashioned to encourage anybody to jump the bridge.

Williamsburg Hoxton

Most Suitable for Twenty-Something's

The hipster British hoteliers' first location in North America pays homage to their very first establishment, which was located in gentrified Shoreditch in East London. This location, a former factory in the heart of

Williamsburg, one of the continent's most stylish neighborhoods, is well-liked by a comparable young, laptop-toting population. It's the place to book for casual-chic since the rooms here maintain the industrial theme while adding flair with art deco accents and the occasional skyline vista.

Sincerely, Tommy

Ideal for a Stay with a Narrative

The experience at "S, T, Eat and Stay" will make you reevaluate all you thought you knew about hostels. Kai Avent-deLeon, the owner, converted her grandmother's Bed-Stuy brownstone into one of Brooklyn's most exquisite concept shops and restaurants. Since then, she has added lodging for visitors, particularly other black women, seeking warmth and safety in addition to design.

Sincerely Tommy was designed as a love letter to the neighborhood, which has welcomed it as an accessible, stylish, and culturally rich place, so it should come as no surprise that it has a homey atmosphere.

R.L. Hotel Brooklyn

Best for Those Looking For A Rising Star

This trendy hotel makes up for its lack of tranquility with the atmosphere. Visitors to this establishment desire to stay far away from the tourist route since it is situated in residential Park Slope, on the boundary of Bushwick and Bed-Stuy. The R.L. gives you a sense of being in a genuine neighborhood; the rooms are small, and you can hear the J train thunder from the neighboring metro station (such is life in the never-ending city). However, a grungy in-house bar that is one of the finest for live music in the neighborhood, a gaming and screening room, and a Brooklyn-centric industrial design all work to lessen the tension.

Wythe Hotel

Best for Location

This eight-story former factory is a Brooklyn hospitality landmark; it was the first luxury hotel to open in the borough back in 2012 and enjoys a prime location in

Williamsburg, benefiting from Bedford Avenue's energy as well as offering spacious rooms with waterfront views of the East River and midtown Manhattan. Nearly ten years later, The Wythe is still a topic of conversation among artistic Brooklynites, who chit chat about everything from the bar's staff turnover to the arrivals and departures of the establishment's fabled parties.

Best for Art, Nu Hotel

This hip hotel in the heart of Brooklyn has earned a reputation as one of the area's most understatedly fashionable establishments. The whole area is decorated in a modern art gallery manner, with flashes of color and texture. Each of the 93 loft-style rooms is distinctive and decorated with various accents, such as hammocks and laser-cut metal headboards. Still, art enthusiasts should focus on the "N.U. Perspective" apartments, which feature expansive murals created by regional artists. However, anticipate no frills; the atmosphere is relaxed and chill.

Hotel McCarren & Pool

Optimal for solo travelers

This quirky, Scandi-style hotel, located on the border of Williamsburg and Greenpoint, close to McCarren Park and some of the borough's most well-known brunch restaurants, does a brisk business in the summer. While the rooftop bar and restaurant are widely known for their vast craft beer menus, the hotel's big outdoor saltwater pool, open from June to October, is crowded with revelers from near and far and DJs playing house music. It's excellent for single travelers and 20-somethings looking to network.

William Vale

Optimal For Vistas

The sleek skyscraper The William Vale sticks out; it was an especially noticeable addition to Williamsburg, a generally flat neighborhood with a solid industrial heritage when it debuted in 2016. Unmistakably contemporary in style and philosophy, with uncommon balconies in a city with little outside space, people flock to this location for breathtaking views. The 60-foot pool, New York's longest pool, and the rooftop bar continue to draw large audiences. Although they provide spectacular views of Brooklyn, most people travel to watch the sunset behind the Manhattan skyline.

Safety Tips for Visitors

Visiting Brooklyn's distinctive culture, architecture, and restaurants is the best way to see it. Keep yourself safe and mindful of your surroundings while you explore. We've compiled a list of safety recommendations to ensure you have the most significant time possible in Brooklyn.

- Trust your gut first and foremost. Find a secure location and talk to a friend or family member about your worries if anything seems wrong.
- When in doubt, remain on the major thoroughfares and near well-lit areas.
- Survey the surroundings before entering any establishment—store, restaurant, or tourist spot. Avoid it and choose another location if it seems shady or risky.
- Remember to store your wallet, pocketbook, and other carry-on belongings in a hotel safe or at home. Take particular care to secure your possessions in these two locations in Brooklyn, as they are prone to theft.

- When strolling around the borough, keep your phone, keys, and wallet in a difficult place to access. Give pickpockets no easy targets, please.
- Watch for any possible dangers, such as hostile individuals or animals. If you don't feel secure or at ease, leave the place and, if necessary, seek assistance.
- Finally, familiarize yourself with local laws and traditions. It includes dressing appropriately, observing curfews, and refraining from taking pictures of official structures or military installations.
- By following these straightforward safety recommendations, visitors to Brooklyn may safely take in the borough's culture, sights, and cuisine. Always follow your gut and be extra cautious to have a hassle-free time in Brooklyn.

Money-saving tips for visitors

Traveling to New York City may be pricey. There are many methods for a tourist to Brooklyn to enjoy them while saving money. Here are some suggestions to help visitors visiting Brooklyn save money:

- Benefit from free activities: Brooklyn hosts several free events all year round. There's always something going on in Brooklyn, from outdoor events to free museum days. Look into the free activities in and around Brooklyn to save a ton of money.
- Take public transportation: Owning a vehicle in Brooklyn may be costly, and the congestion in New York City can be annoying. Using the city's public transit system to far more effective and you can save a ton of money with a Metro card.
- Dine at reasonably priced establishments: Many Brooklyn eateries may be expensive. Fortunately, the neighborhood is home to several inexpensive restaurants. You may get affordable lunches in diners, fast food joints, and other establishments.

- Shop at cheap stores: Stores like Marshalls, T.J. Maxx, and Home Goods are excellent places to discover amazing deals. There are many shops around Brooklyn, so you may get a lot of goods for less than they would cost at traditional retail.
- Visit nearby attractions: Brooklyn is home to a ton of fantastic attractions that you may visit to save money. There are many sites to discover that won't set you back an arm and a leg, ranging from free parks and museums to street art galleries.

Conclusion

Travelers are enthralled by Brooklyn's fantastic combination of ethnic variety, lively neighborhoods, and distinctive vitality, making it stand out globally. This borough provides a wide range of experiences that will leave tourists in amazement and craving more, from famous monuments to little-known jewels.

The artsy vibe that pervades Brooklyn is impossible to resist. The borough is a refuge for artists and fans because of its vibrant art culture. Brooklyn is a rich and ever-evolving tapestry of creative expression that creates a lasting impact, from the well-known street art in Bushwick to the countless galleries in DUMBO.

Beyond the art, each of Brooklyn's neighborhoods has a unique personality, weaving a tapestry of variety. Williamsburg entices the young and the young at heart with its hipster lifestyle and trendy boutiques. With its lovely brownstones and tree-lined avenues, Park Slope provides a tranquil haven from the busy metropolis. And Coney Island enables tourists to indulge their inner kid with its classic amusement park and nostalgic boardwalk.

Bon viveur will be in culinary heaven since Brooklyn's culinary culture is a blend of tastes worldwide. Every bite and budget is catered to by the borough's restaurants, food trucks, and lively markets, which provide anything from classic Italian dining in Carroll Gardens to genuine Mexican cuisine in Sunset Park.

Brooklyn's parks and green areas, such as Prospect Park and Brooklyn Bridge Park, provide fresh air in the city's heart. These outdoor recreation areas allow tourists to get in touch with nature while admiring breathtaking views of the Manhattan skyline, including picnics, running, kayaking, and outdoor concerts.

Brooklyn is a place that captures the spirit of New York City while also preserving its unique individuality. It is a must-visit location for tourists looking for a genuine and educational experience because of its unique neighborhoods, thriving cultural scene, and gastronomic pleasures. Brooklyn promises a voyage that will make an everlasting impression on the hearts and minds of everyone who goes inside its borders, whether it be wandering through the streets of DUMBO, immersing oneself in the art of Williamsburg, or experiencing a variety of delicacies at local cafes.

Made in the USA
Columbia, SC
28 October 2023